Education and Politics

a History of Unintended Consequences
and the Case for Change

Published by

An Imprint of Melrose Press Limited
St Thomas Place, Ely
Cambridgeshire
CB7 4GG, UK
www.melrosebooks.co.uk

FIRST EDITION

Cover designed by Hannah Belcher

ISBN   978-1-912333-06-6 Paperback
978-1-912333-07-3 epub
978-1-912333-08-0 mobi

Printed and bound in Great Britain by:
CMP (UK) Ltd, G3 The Fulcrum, Vantage Way
Poole, Dorset, BH12 4NU

Education and Politics

a History of Unintended Consequences and the Case for Change

David Arnold

Dedication

To all those teachers in secondary schools, whether grammar schools, comprehensive schools, independent schools, sixth form colleges or any other form of secondary school, who have year after year prepared lessons, taught both those who wanted to learn and those who did not, marked work, promoted good learning, given time and energy to a whole range of other activities, maintained good order, undertaken all the various duties which fell to them and cared for both the present and the future wellbeing of their charges.

About the Author

David Arnold was born in Hackney and educated at an elementary school and Christ's Hospital, where he won a history scholarship to Pembroke College, Oxford. Two years in the army and three at Oxford were followed by teaching for three years at Clifton College, Bristol, and by marriage and three children.

For 16 years he was a Head of a History Department, first at a former London grammar school, now Quintin Kynaston, where he wrote a much used textbook, *Britain, Europe and the World 1870–1955*, and then at Stowe School, Buckingham, where he produced the second edition covering 1871–1971.

In 1976 he went to be the headmaster of King George V School, Southport, with the job of turning a boys' grammar school into a mixed sixth form college. After his wife's death he moved in 1983 to be the Principal of the College of Richard Collyer in Horsham, and while there married again.

In retirement he wrote *In the Context of Eternity, a short history of the Christian Church*, which was published in England in 2015 and in the USA in 2017. In 2016 he was elected a Fellow of the Historical Association 'in recognition of a significant contribution to the promotion and knowledge of History'.

His autobiography, *From Hackney to Horsham, a Schoolmaster's Life*, will be published in the summer of 2018.

ACKNOWLEDGEMENTS

I should like to thank all those who in the autumn of 2016 came to the evening course on *Education and Politics* at the College of Richard Collyer, where I gave the series of talks which now form the chapters of this book, and particularly Paul Clarke, a former colleague at Collyer's, first as Head of English and later as Senior Tutor, who presided over each meeting and made sure that all the participants in the course got involved in the discussions following the talks.

I must also thank three old friends, Hilary Anslow, Principal of King George V College from 1992 until 2010, Richard Poulton, Head Master of Christ's Hospital from 1987 until 1996, and Valerie St Johnston, whom I first met when we were at Oxford together and who was later the Head of History at Westminster School from 1987 until 1997, for reading the first draft of the manuscript and offering both encouragement and helpful advice.

Finally, I must thank my wife, Catherine, a former primary school teacher, who tried to ensure that I avoided unnecessary repetition, and that what I wrote on aspects of education about which I knew little was neither too ignorant nor too patronising in tone. I hope she succeeded.

David Arnold

FOREWORD

English secondary education in the early twenty-first century is in a muddle, and has been at least since 1944 and arguably since long before that. Many individual schools and many teachers do a good job, and standards of literacy and numeracy are generally higher than they were a century ago. But we have three problems which are the direct result of the failure of politicians to take effective action. One is the lack a coherent national system. Another is the divide between the independent and maintained sectors. The third is the lack of forms of education which those in their early teens would willingly choose.

We suffer not only from what the politicians have left undone but also from what they have done. Their interventions in secondary education, particularly from 1944 onwards, have done untold damage, so that, for example, thousands of teenagers are subjected to courses which are neither interesting nor useful, our examinations system does not serve the purpose for which it was originally designed, and the inspectorate is more often seen as a threat than as the source of wise counsel.

Large numbers of parents pay substantial fees for something which, at least in principle, is provided free at 'state' schools, and at least some of them do not want the double expense of paying fees and then having their taxes spent on schools for other people's children. Meanwhile, there are people whose children are educated free at public expense but feel that they are getting something substandard. Some people remember nostalgically the good grammar schools we have lost. Others look back with unhappy memories to the secondary moderns they were required to attend.

This book is not an argument for bringing back grammar and secondary modern schools and selection at 11+. Nor is it an attempt to explain how one might achieve the comprehensive ideal. It explains how we have got into the present unsatisfactory position and advocates a fundamental reappraisal of how English education should be organised.

Both Labour and Conservative governments have contributed not only to damaging the maintained sector of secondary education but also to the development of the independent sector. In particular Labour's unintended expansion of the independent sector in the late 1970s has ensured that the independent schools are now seen by both major parties as too good to be abolished. The problem can only be solved by finding a way of integrating the independent schools within a national system so that there is no distinction in law between independent and maintained schools and those very terms come to be both superfluous and meaningless.

Most historians write about events and developments about which they have no direct personal experience. But from Xenophon to Winston Churchill there have always been some who have written about events in which they played a leading part, and many others have given accounts of their own experience when that experience is an interesting though limited part of the great events going on around them. What I want to do is write about the developments which led up to the present unsatisfactory state of secondary education in England from the viewpoint of a foot soldier of English secondary education, and from that position I intend to comment less on my own immediate experience, though that does have some relevance, and more on how our political leaders in all the main parties have lacked a coherent strategy and have made one mistake after another as they floundered in situations in which there was neither a clear strategic objective nor a coherent command structure.

I have made use of the history of six schools of which I had direct experience, three of them independent and three maintained out of the public purse, but I have aimed to do so only where their history throws light on how English secondary education has got into its present state, and how it might be transformed. Chapter 1 explains my relationship with those schools and is more personal than the rest of the book. Only Chapters 2, 3 and 4 are outside my direct personal experience, but they are a necessary preliminary if one is to make sense of what happened from 1944 onwards.

There are three main problems which now need to be resolved. The first, which embraces the other two, is how to create a national system of secondary education which will be of benefit to the whole range of England's teenagers. The second is how to integrate the independent schools within that system on the principle that if you cannot beat them, you need to join them. The third is how to pay for such a system. Someone has to pay. It could be the state, funding everything out of general taxation. It could be individual parents, paying out of residual taxed income. It could be a mixture of the two. What is clear is that high quality secondary education for all cannot be provided on the principle 'Pile 'em in, teach 'em cheap'.

David Arnold
May 2018

'Education is greatest blessing if of best sorts.
Otherwise no earthly use.'
The Tibetan lama, Teshoo, in Rudyard Kipling's *Kim*.

Contents

CHAPTER 1

Prologue

In 1944, the year of the Butler Education Act, when I was ten years old, I left my elementary school, Ray Lodge, in Snakes Lane, Woodford Bridge, in what is now the London Borough of Redbridge, and spent fifty of the next fifty-five years of my life in six secondary schools. For two of the other five years, between school and university, I was in the army and during the next three, at Oxford. There I continued the process begun at school of reading about, thinking about and writing about history, while spending most afternoons rowing up and down the river.

My education at an elementary school had, of course, been free, funded out of the public purse, and at Christ's Hospital, the school I went to in 1944, it was also free, because although it was an independent school, more importantly it was a charitable institution where an essential requirement for entry was that one's parents' income should be sufficiently low that they could not afford to pay fees. For the next eight years I wore a uniform which had scarcely changed since Tudor times, marched to breakfast, chapel, lunch and tea, did physical training at break in the middle of each morning and slept on a horsehair mattress on wooden boards. I learnt Ancient Greek and Latin, played rugby football and cricket, sang hymns and madrigals, and mastered how to fire a Lee Enfield rifle and set a compass for a night march.

It felt a great privilege to be given the opportunities such an education afforded. At that time most boys left Christ's Hospital soon after they reached the school leaving age, which was raised to fifteen in 1947 when the 1944 Education Act was implemented, and many were

1

found jobs in the City of London. Those thought capable of getting open scholarships to Oxford or Cambridge (it was assumed that no child of the hospital would be able to afford to go up as a gentleman commoner) stayed on to be prepared for the Oxbridge examinations and were regularly exhorted in chapel to undertake a life of service to others. I decided to be a schoolmaster.

My first teaching post on coming down from Oxford was at another independent school, this time a very model of an English public school where the virtues of Godliness and Good Learning were cultivated. At Clifton College in Bristol I lived the life of a typical public school master and spent much of my time teaching English, Latin, History and Religious Education to a form of boys aged fourteen to fifteen, but also teaching medieval history to A level candidates. I coached boats on the river, refereed rugby football matches, ran a debating society, became a house tutor, or under housemaster, and somehow found time to get engaged and then married.

While at Clifton I decided that the most worthwhile part of my job was teaching A level History. I also wanted to be my own master as far as teaching History was concerned. So in 1960 I moved out of the independent sector to be head of history at a grammar school in the heart of London. That was Quintin School in St John's Wood, where I taught the O and A level candidates, while others, mostly the headmaster and the chaplain, taught History to the junior forms. As at Clifton I ran a debating society and helped with coaching the school's crews on the river. Of all the schools I was at Quintin was the only one to have a strong rowing tradition. Shortly before I arrived its 1st VIII had just come seventh in the Schools' Head of the River Race.

During my time there our three children were born and I turned myself from a medievalist into someone at home with the history of the nineteenth and twentieth centuries. A book I wrote on modern history was published in 1966, when the children were aged five, three and one, and from a domestic point of view it was a good time to move on.

It was also the year in which the Inner London Education Authority published its plan to make Quintin School part of a comprehensive school. I moved just before that happened, and this time the move was from the maintained sector back to the independent sector.

In 1967 I went to take charge of the History Sixth at Stowe School near Buckingham, and for nine more years taught medieval history to some A level candidates and modern history to others. As at both Clifton and Quintin School I ran the debating society, and in default of a river ran an archery club. Whether at a grammar school or a public school, the work was much the same. But increasingly I got involved in academic management, became the chairman of the curriculum committee and in charge of university entrance, and by the time I was forty-one I had been a head of a history department for fifteen years. I wondered if I really wanted to go on doing the same thing for another twenty. It was time to look for a headship.

The following year I moved yet again between the independent and maintained sectors, becoming the headmaster of King George V School in Southport, with the job of turning it from a large boys' grammar school into a mixed sixth form college. While I was there KGV was reorganized, re-staffed, rebuilt and re-equipped, but after six years there my wife died at the age of only forty-seven. Our children were now twenty-one, nineteen and seventeen, and I felt that I had to make a new start.

By then I was strongly committed to the idea and ideal of the sixth form college as the best solution to the problems thrown up by comprehensive reorganisation, and in 1983 went to take over as principal of the College of Richard Collyer in Horsham. It was the oldest of the schools at which I spent most of my life, having been founded in 1532, twenty years before Christ's Hospital. Just as KGV had changed from being a boys' grammar school into a sixth form college, so had Collyer's. I was fortunate enough to marry again and roughly half way through my sixteen years at Collyer's the college was moved out of the jurisdiction of West Sussex into a new Further Education sector to be in theory an independent college, but in practice funded by a central funding agency rather than by charging fees.

That was in 1992. In 1999, at the age of sixty-five, I retired and it was possible to look back on twenty years of my life spent in independent schools, ten in grammar schools and another twenty in sixth form colleges – though not exactly in that order. I had moved between one sector and the other four times – something which, I fear, is almost impossible in the twenty-first century. All six of the secondary schools where I had spent so much of my life were engaged in much the same activity: that of educating teenagers up to A level at the age of eighteen. What seemed extraordinary as I looked back was that by the end of 2015 the boarding fees at Clifton, Stowe and even at Christ's Hospital were now over £30,000 a year, while at the other three, at Quintin School, now Quintin Kynaston or QK, at King George V College, or KGV, and at Collyer's, it is illegal to charge anything.

The first three are independent schools, and about 7% of English children in any one year are educated in such schools. Boarding fees are generally in the region of £30,000 a year; day school fees are about half that. The other 93% of English children are educated in that wide range of different schools and colleges which have in common the one characteristic that it is illegal for them to charge fees. The average level of funding per pupil is about an eighth of the amount charged by independent boarding schools and a quarter of the amount charged by typical independent day schools.

This raises a number of questions. Why do so many people choose to spend so much money on their children's education when a similar education is provided free at public expense? How do they afford it? Is it a good investment – financially, academically, socially, or in any other way? Why is the discrepancy between independent school fees and the funding per pupil in so-called 'state' schools so great? Is this what one would expect after a century widely portrayed as an Age of Equality, in contrast to the nineteenth century, which has so often been described by historians as an Age of Liberty?

When Benjamin Disraeli in 1845 gave his novel *Sybil* the subtitle *The Two Nations*, he was commenting on the danger of the division between the rich and the poor, 'who are as ignorant of each other's habits, thoughts, and feelings, as if they were dwellers in different zones, or inhabitants of different planets'. Since then successive governments, Liberal and Labour, Coalition and Conservative, have tried to improve the welfare of the mass of the people, but in their attempts to improve education they have unintentionally exacerbated the very problem about which Disraeli warned.

In 1996, a century and a half after the publication of *Sybil*, at a time when 'state' secondary education was widely criticised, even by those satisfied with their own local school, Michael Barber, Professor of Education at London University, produced a book called *The Learning Game*, which the then Leader of the Opposition, Tony Blair, described as 'provocative and timely, illuminating and optimistic'. I read it and sympathised with much of what Barber said. Although his criticism of what had gone wrong with English education was largely limited to the previous twenty years and he ignored completely the problem of the relationship between the independent and maintained sectors of secondary education, he had at least seen the need for change. He hoped for an educational revolution, with a future Labour government providing 'the maximum amount of diversity consistent with equality' to reform the curriculum, the teaching profession and the organisation of the maintained sector of education.

His proposals were influential, but they did not produce the revolution in education which he believed was needed, largely because the fundamental problem of the relationship between the independent and 'state' sectors was ignored. Neither Barber nor any government nor anyone else writing about English secondary education seemed willing to face that problem – still less try to solve it. Throughout some three hundred pages of his book there is scarcely any reference to independent schools. He mentions a conversation between an independent school headmistress and a taxi driver, north London parents arguing over where to send their child to school, and the fact that Harold Wilson, while a Labour prime minister whose government was encouraging comprehensive reorganisation, happily sent his sons to an independent school. But there is not even a hint that the existence of the independent sector constituted a problem.

Anyone might reply to that criticism that since the independent schools educate only about 7% of the children of any one year, consideration of their place in the English secondary education system is irrelevant. But each year roughly half of the places in English universities go to applicants from that 7%, and that is not irrelevant. Nor did Professor Barber have anything to say about the surviving grammar schools and the sixth form colleges, which provide a substantial proportion of those university entrants who are not from independent schools. His concern was to rescue from failure the great mass of all-through 11-18 comprehensive schools, for which there were such high hopes when they were first founded and which, particularly in the inner cities, were by then widely seen as disasters.

Politicians, professors of education, chief inspectors and civil servants produce books, papers, plans and policies in which they talk of driving up standards and suggest new 'initiatives'. The chaotic muddle of England's educational arrangements is accepted and the idea of an integrated national system of secondary education is ignored. They mistakenly assume that the mass of teenagers should be fed a low level academic curriculum. They neglect the need for good technical education. Above all they avoid facing the widening division between the independent and maintained sectors and the need to bring them together.

In 2015 the government's Social Mobility and Child Poverty

Commission produced a report showing that in the previous year 70% of job offers from Britain's top legal, accountancy and financial companies went to graduates who were among the 11% of their year educated either at an independent school (7%) or at a selective state school (another 4%). It was scarcely a surprising finding, any more than that they were inclined to recruit from prestigious universities which took fewer working-class students. After all, employers wanted to recruit the brightest and best of available talent. The leading independent schools now admitted only the rich, clever and socially privileged. Understandably those rich, clever and socially privileged children went on to the more prestigious universities and then into the top legal, accountancy and financial companies.

It was a matter of particular interest to me that the survey included the remaining maintained grammar schools alongside the independent schools. There are only 164 of them left in the whole country, but they are a reminder of a time when the grammar schools and the public schools could for many purposes compete on roughly equal terms.

No rational person could possibly create England's present arrangements for secondary education if starting from scratch. But to that the answer is, of course, that one never does start from scratch. There is always an historical explanation waiting to be found for anything. So it seemed to me that it could be worth seeking to understand the historical process by which we got to the present position. It is an extraordinary story of intermittent political intervention, with those interventions almost always producing unintended consequences. There can be few areas of public life where politicians of all parties have done so much damage, both by what they have done and by what they have left undone.

CHAPTER 2

Chantry and Charity Schools

England has a long history of seeking to provide good education for those who wanted it. As early as 1406 the Statute of Artificers expressed the ideal that 'every man or woman, of what state or condition that he be, shall be free to set their son or daughter to take learning at any school that pleaseth them within the realm'. We fall a long way short of that six hundred years later, particularly in relation to the ideal that people should be free to choose for their children 'any school that pleaseth them'. But through those six hundred years monarchs, bishops, successful business men, some distinguished women, London livery companies and many others have founded and endowed schools, and in more recent times governments have intervened to try to extend education and improve its quality.

In the Middle Ages various schools which taught reading, writing and Latin, and were later called grammar schools, were founded and endowed by pious benefactors, sometimes as chantries, with the intention that the pupils should say prayers for the soul of the founder. Ideally the endowment was large enough that an unbeneficed clergyman could earn money both by saying masses and by teaching in the school. Schools were scattered through the country wherever they happened to be founded, from Rochester in the East, where there appears to have been a school of some sort attached to the cathedral as early as the seventh century, to Ludlow in the West, where a grammar school was founded in about 1200. But some towns did not have any school at all.

There were a few song schools, often attached to cathedrals, and the school at Rochester may have been such a school. At song schools the children were, above all, taught plainsong, but they learnt Latin as well, and at schools such as Eton, Winchester and Magdalen College School, Oxford, they would, for example, be reading such texts as Ovid's *Metamorphoses*. By the end of the Middle Ages the teaching of music was at a very high level. Thomas Tallis, William Byrd and John Taverner, who all wrote what we now call 'early music' in the years before the Reformation, all seem to have been educated in song schools, in which they learnt to sing treble and improvise harmonies and were already composing music while they were still trebles.

Towards the end of the Middle Ages there also developed a number of business schools, where the young learnt the elements of the common law, accountancy, the art of composing letters, and French for legal and commercial purposes. Between them the grammar schools, the song schools and the business schools form a valuable heritage. It is possible to see how that rich variety could have developed into a national system of academic schools, business and technical, or vocational, schools and specialist music schools.

Meanwhile, something of an educational revolution was taking place as a result of the invention of printing and the production of printed books. Although those who could afford it still sometimes employed an unbeneficed clergyman as a tutor for their sons, and such a tutor might even take his young charge on an educational tour of Europe, increasingly it became possible, instead of relying on a private tutor, to 'read', for example, for the Bar. In a wide range of subjects books were able to make up for the lack of adequate teaching, whether by a private tutor or at a school, and so important was reading in education that anyone going up to one of the ancient universities in the late twentieth century was still said to 'read' whatever subject he or she studied – even if it was Mathematics or Engineering.

The will of Richard Collyer, a prosperous London merchant and member of the Mercers' Company, provides a good example of the foundation of an endowed school which was also a chantry. He made his will on 23rd January of 1532 and on 12th March, just seven weeks later, probate was granted, so it seems probable that the will was made on his deathbed. It provided for a free school in Horsham in the county of Sussex where he was born, to educate sixty scholars, children of poor men, who in return for their schooling were to pray his soul. The school was set up so that the *De profundis*, or Psalm 130, should be said for Richard Collyer's soul, for that of his wife, Kateryn, and for all Christian souls at the departing of the school each day. It was also an act of charity, and Richard Collyer wanted 'none to be refused likely to learn'.

In those days the year ran from Ladyday, 25th March, the Feast of the Annunciation of the Blessed Virgin Mary, nine months before Christmas Day, until the following 24th March. So the will was made and probate was granted before the end of the year. Later the dating system was changed so that the year started each 1st January, and that had the effect of making most of the last three months of 1532 into the first months of 1533. It is worth noting the precise date of Richard Collyer's will, because, as it happens, it was a significant moment in English history, just two days before Henry VIII secretly married Anne Boleyn. She had become pregnant and for the sake of the succession to the throne it was important that the child in her womb (it was the future Queen Elizabeth I) should be legitimate.

In 1547, more than a decade later, and a few months after Henry VIII's death, there was passed the Chantries Act, which declared that chantries were based on 'vain opinions of purgatory and masses' and that their endowments should be used instead for such purposes as the 'erecting of grammar schools to the education of youth in virtue and godliness'. Collyer's was in the comfortable position that, although a chantry, endowed to say the *De profundis* for the soul of the founder, it was already a school, and as such it continued.

The government of the school was shared between the Parish of Horsham and the Mercers' Company. The Vicar, the Churchwardens and two honest men of the parish were to choose the Master and the Usher (a second schoolmaster) and also decide which children should be admitted to the school. The appointments of the Master and the Usher needed to be confirmed by the Mercers' Company, which was to pay them and also provide for the building and maintenance of the school out of the income from the property left by Richard Collyer for that purpose. Over the next three and a half centuries the Company regularly paid the Master and Usher and repaired the school when necessary.

For centuries there had been arguments all over the country about who should benefit from the education provided by schools of that sort. At Collyer's it was intended to be 'children of poor men', but in 1540, still in the reign of Henry VIII, when commissioners were considering the future of the grammar school at Canterbury, they wanted 'only gentlemen's children' to be admitted. Archbishop Cranmer did not agree. He wrote to them that 'if the gentleman's son be apt to learning let him be admitted; if not apt, let the poor man's child being apt enter his room'.

Some today would feel that Cranmer did not go far enough, but in some respects we are in a worse position today than then. In the sixteenth century the children of the rich and the poor were often educated together. Now they are more often segregated, and few things reflect the divide between rich and poor in the England of the twenty-first century more vividly than the divisions in the education system.

The reign of Henry VIII is the first time in English history when there appeared to be the prospect of substantial government involvement in education. Henry had plans for the founding of a large number of grammar schools. One was founded in Abergavenny in Wales and another in Coventry, and the school attached to Rochester Cathedral was refounded as the King's School. But those plans faded as Henry wasted the substantial revenues he got from selling off monastic land by engaging in pointless and expensive wars with France. Although at the end of his reign there were a few grammar schools scattered around the country in small towns such as Abergavenny, Horsham, Ludlow and Sherborne, in some large towns, such as Manchester, Birmingham or Liverpool, there was no school at all.

The idea of establishing grammar schools throughout the country was revived in the reign of Henry's son, Edward VI, and that brief reign, from 1547 until 1553, saw the founding of a large number of grammar schools which bore the king's name: in Bath, Birmingham and Bury St Edmunds, for example, and in Southampton, Stratford, Stourbridge and Stafford. They and several more were established. It was an impressive beginning. But it was no more than that. The number of schools founded by the monarch in all subsequent reigns for the next four hundred years does not add up to the number of King Edward VI schools.

The most notable of all Edward VI's foundations was Christ's Hospital. In 1552 the staunchly Protestant Bishop Ridley of London preached a sermon in which he exhorted 'the rich to be merciful unto the poor … and to travail by some charitable way and mean to comfort and relieve them'. That was followed by the founding of a hospital which was intended by the king, the bishop and the Lord Mayor of London to be for 'fatherless children and other poor men's children'. It was the product of a 'dede of pittie', and its central purpose was to provide children such as those who scraped for food in the Houndsditch outside the city walls with 'meate, drink and cloths, lodging and learning and officers to attend them'. It was accommodated in the former house of the Greyfriars, or Franciscans, in Newgate Street, at the western entrance to the City, and once vagrant children had been collected from the streets of London and scrubbed clean, they were provided with 'virtuous education'. Its endowments came to be immensely valuable, largely because so much of the land the hospital owned was in the City of London.

The difference between the mottos of Collyer's and of Christ's

Hospital is worth noticing. Collyer's was founded before the Reformation in England, and its motto was, and still is, the same as that of the Mercers' Company: *Honor Deo* (or 'Honour to God'). Christ's Hospital was founded during the Protestant Reformation, and its motto, in accordance with the XXIVth of the Articles of Religion in the Book of Common Prayer, eschews 'a tongue not understanded of the people' and is in plain English: 'Fear God. Honour the King'.

In a way the difference between those two mottos, both in language and in content, encapsulates the history of the English Reformation over the twenty years between the foundation of Collyer's by a London merchant's will made in 1533 and that of Christ's Hospital by a royal charter of 1553. It is also worth reflecting that the former, although founded by a private individual, is now funded out of the public purse by a body set up by central government, while the latter, though a royal foundation and thus, in a sense, a 'state' school, is entirely independent of the state.

Government intervention of the sort which produced the King Edward VI grammar schools, scattered all over the country, was emulated very little over the next three centuries. Although about a hundred and fifty new schools were endowed in the next hundred years, most of them were founded by Puritan merchants of the City of London, much as medieval barons founded monasteries, in this case with the intention that the children who went to them should be brought up as good Protestants.

As far as central government was concerned, the political tradition which developed in England and lasted through most of the seventeenth, eighteenth and nineteenth centuries was that the government should concern itself with the maintenance of law and order at home, the protection of the country from foreign enemies, and not much else. It fulfilled a few other functions, such as ensuring a stable currency, but generally it intervened little in people's lives and very largely left them free to live those lives as they chose or as they could.

The Church concerned itself with education. So did many private individuals. Sir William Borlase founded the grammar school in Marlowe, Buckinghamshire, which still bears his name, in 1624, and that practice continued. As late as 1886 Quintin Hogg, an Old Etonian businessman and philanthropist, grandfather of the twentieth century Lord Hailsham, founded the Polytechnic Day School in Regent Street in the heart of London. In 1887 Sir Samuel Marling founded the boys' grammar school which still bears his name in Stroud for the sons of those of 'moderate means'. The people who sent their children to these schools wanted something more for them than the elementary education which by 1870 was universal, and they were both willing and able to pay for it, even if they could not afford the fees at one of the recently founded public schools.

Central government had in 1870 introduced universal elementary education up to the age of thirteen, but it had got little further with secondary education than the setting up of two commissions: the Clarendon Commission in 1861, to investigate the finances and management of nine leading schools, all originally charitable foundations but often referred to as public schools, and the Taunton Commission in 1864 to investigate the rest of secondary education in England. But even after those commissions had reported, the government left secondary education to private individuals and groups, to the Charity Commission and to the Church. What is most remarkable about the history of education in England in the half a millennium before the twentieth century is the extent to which private individuals and groups provided so many schools for the general benefit of the community.

Chapter 3

Grammar and Public Schools

All through the seventeenth, eighteenth and nineteenth centuries it was a matter of historical accident whether a particular town had a grammar school or not. Meanwhile, the developing industrial revolution, the consequent social and political changes, and eventually the growth of the British Empire had the effect that there came to be a demand for schools open to the public, as distinct from those private schools which sometimes existed in the household of an aristocrat or a bishop. Entry to the old endowed schools was often restricted to the inhabitants of a particular town and sometimes was specifically for the children of the poor. Now there was increasingly a demand for schools suitable for the sons of those members of the new middle class who were willing to pay for a classical education for their sons and wanted them also to learn gentlemanly conduct. Such schools would be staffed by the sort of clergyman who a generation earlier would have been the private tutor of a young member of the English aristocracy on a Grand Tour of Europe.

An outstanding example of such a school was Rugby, which had been founded during the reign of Queen Elizabeth I as a grammar school for local boys, but in the early nineteenth century was already enrolling boys from further afield who could board during the term with one of the masters. The outstanding example of such a clergyman schoolmaster is Thomas Arnold, who in 1815 became a fellow of Oriel College, Oxford, at the age of twenty, gave up his fellowship four years later in order to get married, served as a clergyman in Laleham, Middlesex, for nine years, finding time to tutor university entrants, and then in 1828, at the age of thirty-three, went to be the headmaster of Rugby, which he transformed into the model of the English public school.

As Headmaster he made clear to the senior boys and to their parents that he valued first, religious and moral principles, secondly, gentlemanly conduct, and thirdly, intellectual ability. The ideals of Godliness and Good Learning which he promoted helped to produce a rise in the esteem in which public schools were held, and that rise in esteem encouraged the process by which some, though very far from all, of England's ancient endowed grammar schools abandoned their original purpose of providing education for local children and instead became public boarding schools for the sons of the landed gentry and the middle classes.

In the 1850s and 60s the small endowed grammar school in Sherborne in Dorset, which had previously provided free schooling to the children of the poor, was gradually changed into a public school, providing education to the children of local farmers and tradesmen. At about the same time the grammar school in the little town of Uppingham in Rutland was opened to all those of the middle classes who could afford the fees to send their sons away to school to board with a housemaster. In 1876 the Laxton Grammar School in the market town of Oundle in Northamptonshire, founded in 1556 by Sir William Laxton and maintained by the Worshipful Company of Grocers, was divided into two separate schools. Laxton Grammar School continued to take local boys, but Oundle School became a public school, and eventually Laxton Grammar became the day boy house of Oundle School.

From one point of view developments such as these could be seen as a great reform. Sherborne, Uppingham and Oundle, and other schools like them, were now providing a classical education for the sons of the new professional and entrepreneurial middle class, mixing those children with the children of the old aristocracy, teaching them to be gentlemen, and providing the nation with a homogenous ruling elite. There was a sense in which these schools existed not so much for the sons of gentlemen as for the fathers of gentlemen. From another point of view it was a process in which the poor were deprived of their endowed schools and the working class were separated off even more than before from the public-school educated middle and upper classes.

That was part of the reason why some ancient endowed schools resisted the change. At Collyer's in Sussex an unsuccessful proposal in 1856 to increase the number of pupils from sixty to a hundred and raise the leaving age to sixteen, was followed by another proposal in 1881, very much in keeping with what was happening all over the country at the time, that the school should take both day and boarding pupils, with the leaving age raised to seventeen and with most parents paying fees – though there would be ten scholarships and twenty free places.

The proposals caused uproar. *The Horsham Free School Defence Association* was formed, led by working men who had themselves been pupils at the school and who believed that the rich and powerful were stealing the inheritance of the poor. Battle continued for years, with a petition to Mr Gladstone, negotiations, public meetings, bargaining and apparent deadlock. The Association had a powerful and popular case. But the school could not stay as it had been for centuries, so after more than two decades of uncertainty new arrangements were approved by *Her Majesty in Council at Her Court at Balmoral* on 15th October 1889.

These new arrangements were necessarily a compromise. With the advent of newly formed local government authorities the previous year, the Mercers' Company would now share the government of the school with the West Sussex Council rather than with the parish, though the Vicar of Horsham remained a governor *ex officio*, and the school would continue to serve the people of Horsham rather than being open to the public generally. It would take both day and boarding pupils up to seventeen, tuition fees would range from £4 to £10 a year, boarding fees would be no more than £40 a year, and the Mercers' Company would contribute £500 a year to the running costs. The Company also provided a capital sum of £3,000, which, together with £2,500 from the sale of the old school house, enabled the governors to have the school rebuilt just north of Horsham Park at a cost of £5,795. The new buildings were officially opened in April 1893.

Similar battles were fought out all over England, in a manner probably not unlike the battles in the twentieth century over proposals for comprehensive reorganization. While some old endowed schools were changed into public schools (Rugby, Sherborne, Uppingham and Oundle are good examples), many more resisted change, and the numerous schools named after Edward VI continued as grammar schools rather than as public schools.

Meanwhile, there was a strong and increasing demand among the landed gentry and the mercantile and professional middle class for public schools, so not surprisingly the middle of the nineteenth century saw several new foundations. Cheltenham, Marlborough and Radley, for example, were founded in the 1840s, Clifton and Malvern not until the 1860s. They were all public schools in the sense that they were open to those members of the public who were able to pay for their sons to be given a classical education and be provided with board and lodging in the house of one of the masters, though some, such as Clifton, took day boys as well.

The first Headmaster of Clifton, J.C.Percival, was another clergyman schoolmaster. He had been a master under Thomas Arnold at Rugby, had imbibed his ideas about Godliness and Good Learning, and was only twenty-eight in 1862 when he began his seventeen year headship of Clifton, during which time he made it one of the country's leading public schools. He left to be the President of Trinity College, Oxford, then from 1887 until 1895 was Headmaster of Rugby, and finally was Bishop of Hereford until 1917. Clifton College was built in a particularly attractive part of Bristol, between the Downs and the Clifton Gorge, and I remember on my first afternoon there as a new schoolmaster in 1957 walking up towards the gorge and coming round the corner to see the astonishing sight of the Clifton Suspension Bridge, built by Isambard Kingdom Brunel and completed in 1864, just two years after the foundation of the school.

One of the most famous of Old Cliftonians was Sir Henry Newbolt, who wrote the poem *Vitaï Lampada* in 1892. It is very much of its time, written at the height of empire, and in its opening refers to the Clifton College Close, the large playing field area overlooked by the main school buildings. The first verse begins: *There's a breathless hush in the Close tonight. Ten to make and the match to win.* It ends: *But his captain's hand on his shoulder smote. 'Play up! Play up! And play the game!'* The second verse takes the reader to a very different situation: *The sand of the desert is sodden red – red with the wreck of the square that broke. The gatling's jammed and the colonel dead.* It ends: *But the voice of a schoolboy rallies the ranks: 'Play up! Play up! And play the game!'*

It is no longer a fashionable poem, but in the early twentieth century it was widely seen as illustrating the way in which a public school education was expected to fit the sons of the upper middle classes to serve their country in the empire and in the army. By then a public school education often appeared to emphasise the importance of playing a straight bat and tackling low more than the virtues of good learning. Clifton had a remarkable school song, with words by Sir Henry Newbolt and the tune by Sir Hubert Parry. The chorus at the end of each verse finished with the words, 'They were great days and jolly days at the best schools of all'.

Field Marshal Earl Haig was an Old Cliftonian, and Sir Arnold Wilson, son of Canon J.M. Wilson, the second Headmaster of Clifton, was educated there before going to Sandhurst. He was awarded a DSO in the First World War and had a distinguished career as a colonial administrator before becoming Member of Parliament for Hitchin from 1933 until 1940. He was killed in 1940 when he was shot down at the age of fifty-six, serving as a rear gunner in Bomber Command.

It fitted with the ethos of the place.

Schools such as Rugby and Clifton were not necessarily what was wanted by some members of the middle classes. Many members of the mercantile middle-class living in central London in the residential area near Regent Street, foreign diplomats living in central London who had no wish to send their sons away to school, and prosperous immigrants who also wanted to keep their sons at home, wanted a good day school in an area where few existed. Thus it was that a Victorian businessman and philanthropist, Quintin Hogg, moved by that zeal for educational improvement which was characteristic of many reformers in the second half of the nineteenth century, founded a school in the centre of London. He was devoted to good works, believing that what was needed was 'not so much a lot of writing about religion as dealing with everything with a religious spirit', and after founding the first Polytechnic in the country as an evening institute in Regent Street, with courses ranging from Hindustani and English for Foreigners to Tailor's Cutting and Carriage Building, he founded a school in 1886.

It was sixteen years since the state had been providing universal elementary education, and the government would not get involved in secondary education for another sixteen. So Quintin Hogg, recognising the urgent need in central London for good secondary education, and appreciating that it did not make commercial sense to leave the Polytechnic's classrooms empty during the day, founded the Polytechnic Day School for Boys. He devoted time and money to developing both the Polytechnic and the Day School, and by the time he died in 1902 he had put at least £100,000 of his own money into them – a vast sum at that time.

The Day School was founded with the clear intention of providing good modern education for the sons of the prosperous middle-class families who lived in the nearby residential area. It was explicitly a 'Middle Class School' in which the fees for teenagers were £2.12s.6d a term – or roughly £2.62 in decimal currency. That was two weeks' pay for some working men, so from 1888 onwards Quintin Hogg provided twelve scholarships a year to enable bright London elementary school boys to have free secondary education.

By the end of the nineteenth century most secondary education was either in endowed grammar schools or in the increasingly large number of public schools. So great was the demand for public schools that, of the eighty-nine in England and Wales at the end of the nineteenth century, fifty-four of them, or 60%, had been founded during that century. Generally speaking academic standards were higher in the leading grammar schools, but the public schools were widely seen as providing an education for 'the whole man', and aspects of that were both admired and copied in many grammar schools, especially in those whose headmasters had been appointed from the staffs of the leading public schools – as many were, and as I was as late as 1976.

The Victorian public school model had a powerful impact on secondary schools, not only in England but also in far-flung parts of the empire. The concepts of the headmaster, the schoolmaster and the school governing body came from the public school model. So did games, prizes, a prefect system and a house system, which could still be a useful way of dividing up a school, even when there were no boarding houses in which the pupils lived. But developments such as these depended on the ideas and actions of individual head teachers and governing bodies. There was no national policy. With hindsight what is remarkable is how well so much developed when governments did not interfere. Governing bodies appointed head teachers who were responsible for the curriculum and for the discipline of both staff and pupils. The head teachers appointed the other members of staff, and between them they created schools admired all over England and in much of the rest of the world.

CHAPTER 4

Towards State Intervention

The founding of grammar schools during the short reign of Edward VI was a brief departure from the English political tradition that the government was expected to maintain law and order at home and protect the nation from foreign enemies, but was not expected to interfere in matters such as education. That tradition continued through the seventeenth and eighteenth centuries, and only in the nineteenth century did governments move tentatively towards involvement in the provision of elementary education, while at the same time trying to avoid involvement in the arrangements for secondary education.

In 1833 a Whig government led by Earl Grey started providing funding for church schools and acquired powers of inspection which in turn led to a measure of parliamentary control. But it was not until 1858 that Lord Derby, at the head of a Tory government, set up a commission under the chairmanship of the Duke of Newcastle to investigate what education was provided for the whole mass of children who, if they went to school at all, usually left at the age of eleven. The commission was asked to consider how it might be possible to provide 'sound and cheap elementary instruction to all classes of the people'. Its recommendations were limited, but they helped to generate an increasing demand for a national system of education, and in 1870, during the first premiership of Mr Gladstone, at the head of a Liberal government, provision was made for universal elementary education up to the age of ten. In characteristic Liberal fashion it was not compulsory. Nor was it free, but arrangements were made for the poor to be excused from paying fees.

Meanwhile, back in 1861, Lord Palmerston, leading a predominantly Whig administration in which Gladstone was Chancellor of the Exchequer, had set up a commission under the chairmanship of Lord Clarendon to report on the finances and management of nine leading schools, after he had received complaints about the conduct of the affairs of Eton College. The schools they looked at were, in order of foundation, Winchester, Eton, St Paul's, Shrewsbury, Westminster, Merchant Taylors', Rugby, Harrow and Charterhouse.

It was at a time when politicians, aware of the increasing demand for universal elementary education, were especially anxious not to be involved any more than was necessary in secondary education. But they were faced with the problem that all nine of the schools which the Clarendon Commission was set up to look at had originally been charity schools, yet now they were charging fees to educate the sons of those members of the upper and middle classes who could afford to pay them.

The Commission, which sat from 1861 until 1864, looked at how each of the schools was run and at the various abuses which had grown up, and as a result of its report the Public Schools Act was passed in 1868, applying specifically to seven of those schools. The reason it applied to only seven of them was that St Paul's and Merchant Taylors' argued successfully that their constitutions made them private rather than public schools and therefore they should not be affected by the proposed legislation.

The most significant effect of the Act was to ensure that the crown, the church and the government should not have any responsibility for the seven schools affected by the Act and that instead each of them should be required to have an independent board of governors. Thus legal force was given to the idea that what were known as 'public schools' should operate entirely independently of the state. The arrangements set up by the Public Schools Act applied in principle only to seven schools, but in practice those arrangements came to be adopted by the whole range of public schools, which for the next century and a half operated outside arrangements set up by subsequent governments for the secondary education of the mass of the population, and still do today.

In 1864, the year in which the Clarendon Commission produced its report, another commission was appointed, this one under the chairmanship of Lord Taunton, to examine the rest of secondary education in England, most of which was in the many endowed grammar schools founded over some centuries.

Part of the reason for politicians starting to take an interest in education at this time was that another issue occupying their attention was the question of the further extension of the right to vote, and in the context of Disraeli's Second Reform Bill of 1867, which proposed to give the vote to most working-class men in towns, the Liberal politician Robert Lowe, while opposing the proposal in the House of Commons, spoke to his fellow Members of Parliament about the need to 'prevail on our future masters to learn their letters'. But after the bill was enacted, and although he was Chancellor of the Exchequer and then Home Secretary under Gladstone from 1868 until 1874, the government of which he was a member did remarkably little to take up the idea that 'we must educate our masters'.

The Taunton Commission reported in 1868 on the uneven distribution of schools through the country, on the frequently poor education provided, the lack of science and modern languages, the misuse of endowments and on the fact that there were only thirteen girls' secondary schools in the whole country. It recommended the setting up of an integrated national system of secondary education based on the existing endowed schools. But its recommendations were not implemented, according to Matthew Arnold because 'the upper class do not want to be disturbed in their preponderance, or the middle class in their vulgarity'.

Whatever the reason for the failure of any government during the last thirty years of the nineteenth century to develop a national system along the lines recommended by the Taunton commission, one consequence of the continuation of the fragmented arrangements which developed without any coherent national plan was that in the twentieth century hardly any session of parliament went by without some measure to patch up, modify or extend the continuingly inadequate and unsatisfactory arrangements for secondary education. What Mr Gladstone's government provided in 1869, the year after the Taunton Commission reported, was a typical piece of nineteenth century Liberal legislation. The Charity Commission was empowered to draw up new schemes of government for existing schools, but it was not required to do so. Where it did draw up a new scheme, the Act made ample provision for local people to obstruct any change.

Hence the struggle over Collyer's. The Charity Commission moved to draw up a new scheme of government, the Mercers' Company lawyer argued that there was no need to do so, and for some years the matter lay dormant. There were two very different views about the future. Some looked for an expanded school, with fee-payers and boarders, an extended curriculum and a higher leaving age; others valued the school as it was and saw it as existing to provide a basic education for the children of the poor. That was in line with the view of the Mercers' Company, which provided the school premises and paid the Master and Usher. The Company had no wish to incur the obligations which could result from setting up a significantly larger public school, so it opposed change. In 1876 the Charity Commission threatened to challenge the Mercers' Company at law over the way it had disposed of Richard Collyer's legacy, but it did not pursue this. New arrangements were at last approved in 1889, and the school was rebuilt on a new site in 1893.

The official name was now 'the Horsham Grammar School founded by Richard Collyer' – though local people continued to call it 'Collyer's'. By the twentieth century the number of pupils was just over a hundred and pupils were starting to win open scholarships at Oxford and Cambridge colleges. Then came the First World War, which took a toll of fifty-one lives from the old boys of what was a small grammar school in a West Sussex market town.

Less than a decade after the rebuilding of Collyer's the Almoners of Christ's Hospital decided that the London site in Newgate Street was too constrained for the school to operate effectively and they used their very considerable assets to build a grand new school for boys on a site near Horsham and also established a separate girls' school in Hertford. Christ's Hospital was neither a public school nor a grammar school and had been described by the Taunton Commissioners as *sui generis* – 'of its own sort', or to quote a later paraphrase, 'a school like no other'. It was above all a charitable foundation, which fulfilled that function after 1902 by providing both a boys' and a girls' school for children in need.

Income from investments and from property sustained the two schools separately through most of the twentieth century and enabled the Almoners to continue the charitable purpose and give the children a first-rate education. The hospital still provided the children it cared for with 'meate, drink, cloths, lodging and learning', and the boys still wore a uniform which had hardly changed since the hospital was founded: a long blue coat down to the ground, with silver buttons and a loose girdle (or belt) resting somewhere between the hips and the knees, grey knee breeches, also with silver buttons, yellow stockings (or socks) and black shoes, and hanging over the front of the coat a pair of bands such as were once worn by Protestant preachers. The Duke of Cambridge, as President in the late nineteenth century, gave the very good reason for keeping the traditional Tudor uniform, that 'it prevents lads of a higher class entering Christ's Hospital … keeping it as a charitable institution instead of it being an ordinary Public School'.

Both the rebuilding of Collyer's in Horsham and the building of the Christ's Hospital boys' school a few miles to the south-west took place without any involvement by the government. Central government was so concerned with the two dominating issues of Ireland and the Empire in the later years of the nineteenth century that it largely neglected the need for social reform at home.

But that was gradually changing. Lord Salisbury's Conservative government of 1886–92 devised a system of local government in 1888, with England and Wales divided into sixty-two administrative counties, and in 1889 it made technical education the responsibility of those new local government authorities. His Unionist government of 1895–1902 started to provide grants to some endowed grammar schools and in 1899 it set up a Board of Education to co-ordinate the various different aspects of education and raised the school leaving age to twelve. But that was all.

English secondary education had developed in a piecemeal fashion and at the beginning of the twentieth century England had an extraordinary variety of different sorts of secondary school: public, private, proprietary and preparatory schools, for example, as well as grammar and endowed schools, church schools, grade schools, central schools and monitorial schools, with several of these categories overlapping. The two principal categories of secondary school, and those which were most admired both at home and abroad and had developed with little government intervention, were the public schools and the grammar schools. The leading public schools had considerable social caché; academic standards were higher in the leading grammar schools.

In 1902 Salisbury's successor, A.J.Balfour, gave local education authorities some responsibility for elementary education and for the planning and provision of secondary and technical education. But there was no move towards developing a national system. For example, the Education Act of that year provided that, where a grammar school already existed, the local authority would contribute to its running costs, and where there was no grammar school, the local authority could decide to found one. But equally the local authority could decide not to found one.

The Act also set up a difference in law between the old endowed grammar schools and the new ones founded by local authorities: the former were 'aided', while the latter were 'maintained'. At that stage it was a distinction without any visible difference, but it was the beginning of a process whereby successive administrations dealt with issues piecemeal and gradually produced ever more complicated administrative arrangements until even those whose job was to operate them quite clearly did not understand the complexities.

From 1902, in accordance with the provisions of the Balfour Education Act, the running costs of Collyer's, though not any buildings costs, were paid by the West Sussex County Council, and those of the Polytechnic Day School in Regent Street were similarly paid by the London County Council. Christ's Hospital, as a particularly wealthy charity, and Clifton College, as a public school, continued to pay their own running costs, so they remained independent. But, meanwhile, the first tentative step had been taken, even if unintentionally, to bring both Collyer's and the Polytechnic Day School within what came to be called 'the state system' – even though it was not run by the state and was not a system.

In 1907 the Liberal government made financial arrangements for grammar schools to provide a quarter of their places free to children from elementary schools on the basis of a scholarship examination taken at the age of ten, and the combination of the founding of new grammar schools with the provision of more free places had the effect that between 1904 and 1925 the number of grammar schools in England more than trebled, from 491 to 1,616, and the number of pupils nearly quadrupled, from 85,000 to 334,000.

During the First World War the distinguished Liberal historian H. A. L. Fisher was brought into the Coalition government as President of the Board of Education. He introduced a Bill, which, as the Education

Act of 1918, ensured free elementary education for all, raised the school leaving age to fourteen and further encouraged local education authorities to found more grammar schools, take responsibility for them, and extend the number of free places. The measures still fell a long way short of establishing a national system of secondary education such as had been recommended by the Taunton Commission, and expenditure on education was massively reduced in 1922 when a committee presided over by Sir Eric Geddes reported on how to cut government expenditure 'with an axe'. But at least in principle it was a significant step forward. It also marks the beginning of a half-century which continued into the 1960s and can be thought of as the Golden Age of the English grammar school.

CHAPTER 5

Between the Wars

An early example of the expansion of grammar schools encouraged by the Fisher Education Act of 1918 was the founding in 1920 by the burgesses of the self-governing County Borough of Southport, then in Lancashire, of a boys' grammar school. It began in buildings used during the war as a military hospital. In 1926 it moved into a new and impressive building two miles inland and became King George V School.

The building became the model for other grammar schools built in Lancashire during the 1930s and the school became something of a model of academic excellence in the north-west. It conformed to the developing and widespread practice among grammar schools of having houses within which boys were encouraged to co-operate with each other for communal success, both at work and at games. It was unusual in that, while there were communal prizes and trophies, no boy was ever rewarded with an individual prize either for work or for games.

These were the days when the grammar school was widely seen as a means of social mobility by which boys could start climbing the steps of the educational and social ladder. Middle-class parents were pleased to pay the fees of four guineas a term (a guinea was twenty-one shillings, or one pound and one shilling, and guineas always sounded somehow more upmarket than pounds) and clever working-class boys could win a free place in a scholarship examination at the age of ten.

Scholarship boys entering the school at ten were well established by the time the main intake of eleven-year-olds arrived a year later. Many of them would go into the express stream, which took School Certificate a year early, and would then stay on after taking Higher

Certificate to take the Oxbridge scholarship examinations. The sixth form was increasingly the pride of the school, and was seen as a natural stepping stone to university.

In 1926, the same year that the boys' grammar school in Southport became King George V School, Lord Eustace Percy, President of the Board of Education in Baldwin's Conservative government of 1924–29, made an attempt to sort out the administrative confusion which had resulted from some grammar schools receiving funding from central government, some receiving financial aid from their local authority and some getting income from both. It was decided that those grammar schools which owned their own buildings and land could either receive a 'direct grant' from the government each year in return for providing a proportion of free places, or they could have their running costs paid by their local education authority, while remaining responsible for their own buildings, in which case they would be classified as 'voluntary aided'.

Other more recent grammar schools which had been founded by a local authority and were often referred to as 'county' schools were classified as 'maintained'. Thus for administrative convenience and in principle to provide something simpler than the developing confusion, the grammar schools were divided into three categories: direct grant, aided and maintained. To most people these distinctions were invisible, and they made little or no difference to the day to day running of a school. But the hidden differences, however invisible to teachers and taught alike, had potential for future trouble.

A related problem arose from the belief among politicians and civil servants that every school needs a governing body. Both public schools and old grammar schools had them, so when grammar schools were set up by local authorities, they were given governing bodies, even though the ultimate authority rested in practice, though not in appearance, with the local authority. Again, that was a trivial and entirely unimportant matter for many years, but in the 1960s and the

1970s the issue of whether a majority of the members of a school's governing body was appointed by its own foundation, as in the case of 'aided' and 'direct grant' schools, or by the local authority, as in the case of 'maintained' and yet another category of 'controlled' schools created in 1944, came to be a matter of immense importance affecting the nature and even the very existence of the school.

The demand for new secondary schools after the First World War did not only apply to grammar schools. Many public schools were seriously oversubscribed, so there was a demand for new ones both from parents and from hard-pressed headmasters of preparatory schools, who were finding it difficult to place even some of their most talented pupils. In the light of this a group of men formed a committee with the express intention of establishing a new public school intended to take its place among 'the first six in the country' (It is worth speculating on which would at that time have been perceived to be 'the first six'), and in 1922 they acquired Stowe House, the former home of the Dukes of Buckingham, together with 750 acres of landscaped gardens and all the temples and monuments, for £34,500.

The school they founded had a number of interrelated advantages. First, and most obvious, was its setting in Stowe House and the landscaped gardens, with a magnificent approach along a straight mile long, tree-lined avenue from Buckingham to the Corinthian Arch, which was a gift from a group of Old Etonians. The next advantage was its first headmaster, J.F. Roxburgh, of whom Noel Annan, later Lord Annan and Vice Chancellor of London University, said that 'in the history of the public schools he will stand out as the man most responsible after the First World War for civilising their outlook'. A third advantage was that already in the 1920s many parents from the gentry and what may be called the intellectual middle class were dissatisfied with the prevailing ethos of the great public schools.

In the late nineteenth century the Godliness and Good Learning which had been so successfully promoted by Thomas Arnold at Rugby had often been replaced later in the century by an ethos of muscular Christianity in which team games were seen to be especially important in forming character. Tackling low and playing a straight bat were apparently regarded as the supreme virtues. After the horrors of the First World War many mothers wanted a more civilised educational environment for their sons. Stowe, with J.F.Roxburgh as headmaster, was ideally suited to provide the sort of education they wanted. Academic work, art, drama, music and a variety of sporting activities, not just team games, could flourish in a relaxed environment which had something of the flavour of a country club.

In the same year as the foundation of Stowe another public school, Canford, was founded and located in the private country house known as Canford Manor, the former home of Sir John Guest, and set in three hundred acres of grounds on the banks of the River Stour in Dorset. Five years later Bryanston was also founded and was housed in the former home of Lord Portman, set in four hundred acres of Dorset countryside. Both Canford and Bryanston had the same advantage as Stowe, though on a smaller scale and significantly further from London, of having a grand central building set in acres of attractive countryside.

There was no shortage of parents who could afford the fees. Only Eton charged as much as £245 a year, Rugby's fees were £200, and Stowe, Canford and Bryanston could afford to charge less than that. That needs to be seen in the context of what money was worth at the time. Many men earned less in a year than the fees of the leading public schools. My own father's pay throughout the 1930s was £3 a week, or £156 a year, and that was not enough to afford even the typical day boy fees of, perhaps, £5 a term at a grammar school. Public school fees were likely to be more than ten times that amount.

It is also worth appreciating that most young people in those years left school for work at fourteen. My father, born in 1906, had left school in 1919 at thirteen and started work as a chaff cutter at just the time that the school leaving age was raised to fourteen. Even some boys and girls at grammar schools had to leave at fourteen because their parents could not afford to keep them there. Only the relatively prosperous sent their children to boarding public schools and kept them there until the age of seventeen or eighteen.

Those who could afford to do so usually conformed also to the practice of sending their sons to be educated at a preparatory school from the age of about seven or eight, before going on to a public school at about thirteen. In the years between the wars both the prep. schools and the public schools were sufficiently well regarded that there was a general expectation among the aristocracy, the gentry and many of the middle class that their sons should attend one of them.

Many had been founded in the nineteenth century, so that country gentlemen, clergy, solicitors, local tradesmen, bank managers, officers in the armed forces, civil servants and colonial officers could send their sons, though not yet their daughters, first to acquire Godliness and Good Learning and later what was often described as a public school education of 'the whole man'. It was still usual for people of that sort to send their sons away to school, and many of them could afford to do so.

The distinction between public and grammar schools was not entirely clear, especially in the case of day schools. Manchester Grammar School was clearly a grammar school. So was King Edward VI, Birmingham. But what about St Paul's in London or Merchant Taylors'? They had argued successfully at the time the Clarendon Report was published that they were not public schools, and both were day schools. But many parents, pupils and members of staff would have been offended a few years later if someone had suggested that they were not public schools. The differences between public, private and grammar schools were still very largely a matter of perception.

Public school influence can often be seen in the years between the wars in the way some grammar schools developed. Between 1922 and

1926 the Revd Wilfrid Peacock, who had previously taught at both Uppingham and Cheltenham, was the headmaster of Collyer's in Horsham, and those four years saw the school 'reorganised on modern public school lines'. In his brief headship Peacock introduced a house system, prefects, a school magazine, an Old Boys' Association, a school library, a chapel, Prize Giving and the annual celebration of Founder's Day. Then his successor, Philip Tharp, who came to Collyer's from teaching at Wellington College, was headmaster for thirty years of outstanding success from 1926 until 1956, right in the middle of that remarkable half-century after the First World War which saw grammar schools flourish all over England.

In the years between the wars public schools such as Clifton and Stowe typically charged fees of between £150 and £200 a year, while day schools such as Collyer's in Horsham, the Polytechnic Day School in Regent Street in the heart of London, and King George V School in Southport usually charged about a tenth of that amount. Christ's Hospital, as a charitable institution described by the Taunton commissioners as *sui generis*, or unique, provided free education for children whose parents could not afford to pay anything. Some, both boys in Horsham and girls in Hertford, were the children of clergy or indigent artists or members of the gentry or the middle classes who had fallen on hard times, and they were not necessarily particularly bright. Others were clever working-class children. What they had in common was that they all came from homes with low incomes.

The most obvious difference between the grammar schools and the public schools remained the fact that the former were largely for day pupils, for whom they charged fees usually in the range £15–£20 a year, while the latter were largely boarding schools, charging from £81 a year at the bottom of the fee range up to £245 at Eton. Only four public schools charged more than £200 and only three less than £100. Most, more than two-thirds, charged fees of between £150 and £200 a year. The difference between grammar school and public school fees is partly accounted for by the fact that boarding education necessarily costs more than day. But the difference, a ratio of about 10:1, and the tendency for it to exacerbate social divisions, was a matter of public and political concern.

In the 1920s a common attitude was that it was wonderful when a bricklayer's or bus-driver's son won a free place at a grammar school. By the Second World War rather more people were suggesting that it was scandalous that so few bricklayers' or bus-drivers' sons got places at grammar schools, and as England went into the Second World War only 2% of the nation's children in any one year were receiving free secondary education and the provision of technical education was almost non-existent.

There were three significant problems which needed to be faced. One was the lack of adequate schooling for most girls. The second was the lack of secondary education for most of the working class, who almost all went out to work when they reached the age of fourteen. The third was the social divide between the public schoolboy, who was perhaps increasingly inclined to regard himself as 'upper class', as distinct from the grammar schoolboy, who was usually 'middle class' and sometimes, in the case of scholarship boys, 'working class'. The first problem could be solved by founding girls' schools or by accepting the idea of co-education. The lack of secondary education for most of the working class would ideally have been solved by a combination of further expansion of the grammar schools and the provision of technical schools with a wide range of courses. The problem of the social divide was more difficult.

CHAPTER 6

The 1944 Education Act

Back in 1868 the Taunton Commission had recommended that there should be a national system of secondary education based on the example of the endowed grammar schools. The chance was missed. Grammar schools and public schools continued to be founded and to flourish, but the difference between them as expressed by the fees they charged was increasingly seen as a cause of social division, and it became a matter of such concern to politicians of all parties that during the Second World War a committee chaired by Lord Fleming was asked to consider what could be done about it.

When the Fleming Committee reported in June of 1944 it recommended integrating all the public schools within a national system of secondary education. But the publication of the report coincided with the Anglo-American invasion of Normandy, and its recommendations were first ignored and then generally forgotten. I remember it because the report came out three months before I left my elementary school at the age of ten to go to Christ's Hospital, and my father, then a troop sergeant in the army, bought a copy of it which I read (some of it at least), kept and still have.

Instead of implementing the recommendations of the Fleming Report parliament presented the nation with the 1944 Education Act, which was passed with cross-party agreement and hailed as a great reform. But the theoretical foundation on which it was built was seriously flawed and the manner in which it was implemented generated problems. It was based on a profoundly misguided view of society held by politicians and civil servants who had mostly been educated at Oxford.

The influence of a public school and Oxford education on English educational policy is difficult to overestimate. From 1870, when universal elementary education was introduced, until 1963 there were eleven permanent secretaries in charge of education. All went to Oxford, and although the first two were Scots and educated in Scotland, all the rest went to English public schools. During the same period there were forty-three political heads of education (almost four times as many!), of whom thirty went to public schools, while eighteen of them went to Oxford and half of the rest to Cambridge.

Whether one read Classics or History at Oxford, one was sure to discover from Aristotle that men (women did not come into it) could be divided into three categories: leaders, artisans and slaves. That led to the assumption that children who were judged to be future leaders by virtue of their intellectual ability should go to a grammar school, if they had not already by virtue of their social status and their parents' wealth gone to a preparatory school, en route to a public school. Those who were by nature destined to be artisans should be provided with technical education. The great majority, by nature suited to be members of the slave class, though no one openly spoke of it that way, needed to be provided with a modern form of secondary education suited to their lack of ability.

This so-called tripartite system was not embedded in the Act. It was embedded in the minds of those who devised and implemented it, and it deprived the great mass of parents of any choice over the form of education provided for their children. Untold thousands of parents who in the past had been pleased to pay to send their child to a grammar school, were no longer allowed to do so. The state, or rather officials employed by local education authorities, would decide on the form of education each child should have.

During the war against the tyranny of Nazi Germany the British people had, paradoxically but understandably, accepted a large measure of state control, but now, less understandably since they had been fighting for freedom, they accepted continuing state control with little complaint and on a far larger scale than they ever had in the past. To many of them it seemed wonderful that every child in the country was now to be offered free secondary education. It would have seemed churlish to question the nature of that education or the decisions about where each child should go to school.

No attempt was made to integrate the public schools within the national system. Those parents who could afford to pay public school fees were able to keep their children separate from the *tripartheid* system in a form of *apartheid* based not on race but on wealth. Thus, instead of reducing the divisions between the social classes, the arrangements imposed by the 1944 Act increased the very social divisions which had led to the setting up of the Fleming Committee.

The implementation of the 1944 Act was left to local education authorities, which were required to provide secondary education for all, taking account of 'their different ages, abilities and aptitudes'. Since grammar schools already existed, that was widely interpreted as meaning that they should provide grammar school education for the academically most able, technical education for those with technical aptitude, and a 'modern' form of secondary education for those lacking either academic or technical aptitude.

In practice there were too few grammar school places for those whose parents would have chosen that form of education. With little money available for a building programme, the decision about how many grammar school places to provide was usually made by counting how many places were already available. The result was that there was far less expansion of grammar school education than would have been desirable, while by 1956 the percentage of children deemed suited to a grammar school education varied from one area of England to another from as high as 40% (and in parts of Wales it was as high as 60%) to as low as 10%.

Meanwhile, a form of assessment known as the 11+ selection procedure was adopted throughout the country. Children were examined in English, Maths and Intelligence (which meant a talent for passing intelligence tests) and their performance was claimed to be a reliable indication of their suitability for one form of education or another. It was not. The 11+ was a competitive examination for the available grammar school places. Those who passed went to a grammar school. Those who failed were almost all sent to a secondary modern school, because in most of the country there were no technical schools to go to. More girls failed than boys simply because there were fewer grammar school places for them. The historian A.J.P.Taylor suggested that one should 'run away to sea rather than go to a secondary modern', and many parents who found it difficult to pay the fees of a private school nevertheless did so to save their children the humiliation of going to a sec. mod.

Education authorities deprived many children of a grammar school education because they had too few available places. They also deprived them of a technical education by failing to build technical schools. Most teenagers could have learnt to type and cook and drive as well as becoming both literate and numerate. Many could have acquired qualifications as mechanical or aeronautical engineers, as accountants and bookkeepers, as electricians and as plumbers, as hairdressers, as photographers, or, indeed, a combination of such skills. They could have had useful work experience, and just as much as their contemporaries studying academic subjects, they could have played football and cricket and engaged in a whole range of recreational activities.

But England had seriously neglected technical education in the previous century and continued to do so, and that continued neglect not only deprived young people of a worthwhile education but also had the effect that Great Britain was not only failing to compete successfully with many so-called 'developed' countries but was also losing ground in manufacturing to what were thought of as Third World countries. So few technical schools were built that as late as 1958 fewer than 4% of children were being educated in them.

Most children needed a choice between the academic education provided in grammar schools and the technical education which should have been provided in technical schools. Both of those forms of education needed to be something which the children and their parents valued, for which they would be willing to pay whatever was required, in so far as they could afford it, and for which a child would, if necessary, walk miles every day.

What most got in their underfunded secondary modern schools, often in dilapidated buildings, was a poor quality academic curriculum suited neither to their own needs nor to those of the country as a whole. Large numbers of English children, after being humiliated by being told that they were not suited to an academic curriculum, were provided with just that sort of curriculum but at a low level. Too often they were inoculated against literature by being required to read books beyond their comprehension. Some never entered a theatre throughout a long lifetime because at school they had had to copy out lines of Shakespeare as a punishment. Others were inoculated against Mathematics by being given no explanation of the mechanical tasks they were required to perform, against Physics by being taught by someone who had not studied the subject beyond the age of sixteen, against History by having to copy out boring notes and against all religion by having to sit through tedious lessons or assemblies in which thought was discouraged. They could have benefited from vocational courses, but instead were presented with academic courses which were neither interesting nor relevant to their needs, and they were required by law to put up with it. It could easily be seen as an extended punishment for failing the 11+.

The one significant change in some secondary modern schools from the elementary school from which they had been formed was that they now had fewer clever children than before, because more of the academically brightest were sent to a grammar school. What happened can be illustrated by reference to the elementary school I attended in what is now the London Borough of Redbridge. Before and during the war I went to the infant and junior departments at Ray Lodge, in Snakes Lane, Woodford Bridge, and have good reason to be grateful for the elementary education it provided for children up to the age of eleven. At ten a few boys and girls went to one of the local grammar schools, but most went on a year later to finish their elementary education at the senior school, known as St Barnabas because it was in St Barnabas Road near Woodford Station.

The implementation of the 1944 Education Act in 1947 theoretically changed that, but the idea that there was a significant change was something of a fraud. Those who failed the 11+ still went to St Barnabas, but the curriculum was a low level form of just the sort of academic education for which they had been judged to be unsuited and was not significantly different from what had been provided when it was the senior section of an elementary school. It was no worse than in the rest of the country. But that is only to say that secondary education in maintained schools in England after the Second World War, other than in grammar schools, was not significantly better than what was provided in elementary schools before the war. Not only was the curriculum inappropriate for many of the children. Trying to teach it was dispiriting for many of the teachers.

Matters were made even worse by the raising of the school leaving age to fifteen in 1947. That resulted in 1949 in a national Hut Operation for the Raising of the School Leaving Age, with 6,838 H.O.R.S.A. classrooms being provided by local authorities all over the country, so that those who had to stay at school for another year were trapped in them while someone tried to keep them in order as they fretted against what often felt like imprisonment. It was ludicrous. In a country in which many people paid large sums of money for good education, those whose parents could not afford to do so were held compulsorily for yet another year in schools which gave them poor academic education and no training in useful skills. Understandably they resented it.

One of the tragedies of the attempt to extend secondary education to all in the 1940s was that in the austerity of the post-war world it was seriously underfunded. That helps to explain why there were too few grammar school places and why the technical schools were not built. There was also a short term financial advantage to many local authorities in not having to provide for those children who went to fee-paying schools. Meanwhile, such limited funding as was available tended to go to the grammar schools, which were viewed with pride, rather than to the 'sec-mods', which were seen as problems by politicians and education officers alike.

The 1944 Act was proclaimed as a great step forward, and more working-class children than ever before had free places at grammar schools. But there was a sense in which it was a time bomb which would explode in a generation's time. The abolition of fee-paying places combined with the ruthless segregation imposed by the 11+ had the effect that most parents now had little say in where their children would be educated. Many resented the humiliation their child had suffered by failing the 11+ and paid for them to go to a local private school instead of to a 'sec-mod'. Paradoxically the provision of free secondary education for all stimulated the expansion of the independent sector.

The exclusion of the public and private schools from the provisions of the 1944 Education Act, the lack of choice for children and parents about which sort of school they should go to, the way local authorities were left to implement it in different ways, the inadequate provision of grammar school places, the lack of technical schools, the pretence that the 11+ examination selected children for the form of education best suited to their ability, the inappropriate curriculum at 'sec-mods' – all this generated massive discontent which was given expression when the next generation grew up. All over the country people were determined that their children should not be treated as they had been. No wonder they demanded change! No wonder many demanded that all children should be educated together in 'comprehensive' schools!

CHAPTER 7

Grammar Schools and the 11+

If the Battle of Waterloo was won on the playing fields of Eton, and if the young men who led their infantry platoons to victory in the First World War often had little training other than maintaining order in the dayrooms and dormitories of public schools, the Second World War was in some measure won in the classrooms and laboratories of the grammar schools. While young men from the public schools still commanded platoons in the Brigade of Guards and squadrons in cavalry regiments which were now equipped with tanks, there were large numbers of former grammar school boys in positions of responsibility in the Royal Engineers and in the Royal Artillery, in signals and in transport, flying as sergeant pilots in the Battle of Britain and as bomber crew over Germany, serving in the Royal Navy and in the merchant service.

In the two decades after the Second World War the grammar schools flourished, provided high quality academic education, and were generally highly regarded. One of the few merits of the 1944 Act was that it resulted in enough of an increase in the number of grammar school places that it was possible in the post-war years to take the view that it was wonderful that so many clever young working-class boys and girls were now getting a free grammar school education.

A problem which had existed from 1926 onwards was that there were three different categories of grammar school: 'direct grant', 'voluntary aided' and 'maintained'. Now the confusion was made worse by adding a fourth category of 'voluntary controlled' schools. These were grammar schools which had previously been 'aided' but now needed their local authority to provide new buildings. They, like the 'maintained' schools, had to accept a majority of local authority governors on the governing body, while the 'direct grant' and 'voluntary aided' schools had a majority of foundation governors who were thus in a position to outvote the governors appointed by the local authority. The confusion was increased still further by a provision in the 1944 Act allowing the direct grant schools to charge fees, while it was illegal for any of the others to do so.

Few people cared or even knew about these technicalities of school governance, and neither the pupils nor even most members of staff would have known into which category their school happened to fall. They would find in the 1960s and 1970s, as the national battle over comprehensive reorganisation was fought out, that it mattered very much indeed.

Many of those schools, whatever their administrative category, were demonstrably very good. Collyer's in Horsham, which was 'voluntary aided', Quintin School in St John's Wood, which was 'voluntary controlled', and King George V School in Southport, which was 'maintained', are three examples of that excellence. With scant resources other than blackboard and chalk, well-thumbed textbooks, and above all well qualified teachers, such schools got on with transforming the lives of their pupils.

The Horsham Grammar School founded by Richard Collyer grew substantially between the wars and for thirty years, from 1926 until 1956, flourished under an outstanding headmaster, Philip Tharpe, usually known as PAT. It is a measure of the growth of the school and of the town of Horsham that the number of Old Collyerians killed in the Second World War, seventy-two, was significantly more than the fifty-one killed in the First. Just after PAT's retirement the school benefited from a substantial legacy which provided Collyer's with a range of new buildings, including a headmaster's house. As a 'voluntary aided' grammar school it needed to be able to provide half the cost out of its own endowment, with the other half coming from central government.

Shortly afterwards this amount was significantly reduced to 25% and later still to 15%, as the government tried to encourage new building. The school no longer took boarders and it was no longer allowed to charge fees. The running costs were paid by the West Sussex Local Education Authority, but the Mercers' Company rather than West Sussex still controlled the Governing Body.

Quintin School had flourished as the Polytechnic Day School in Regent Street until the outbreak of the Second World War required its evacuation to Somerset. When it returned at the end of the war, the Polytechnic, previously an evening institute and now on its way to becoming the University of Westminster, needed the accommodation in Regent Street all through the day. The years of austerity after the Second World War made it difficult to acquire a new building in central London. So for a decade the pupils in their green blazers with red braid could be seen walking from one lesson to another in various buildings in Soho – one of them immediately opposite the Windmill Theatre. After the school had spent a decade in temporary accommodation, the London County Council provided both a site and a building in St John's Wood, the name was changed to *The Quintin School*, though the definite article was soon dropped, and in 1956 it moved into its new buildings.

The headmaster from 1937 until 1958 was a Dr Worsnop, who came from being a Senior Lecturer in Physics at King's College, London, and was in post for only two years before he led the school to evacuation in Somerset for the six years of war, coped with the problems of temporary accommodation in Soho for another decade, and then was headmaster in St John's Wood for just two years from 1956 until his retirement. He left behind a well-built, well-equipped and well-staffed grammar school in an attractive area of central London. It was one of the very few grammar schools in the country whose rowing VIIIs, based at Chiswick, were able to compete successfully with the best public school crews, and both staff and pupils took pride in the fact that its Sea Scout Boat, *The Quintinian,* had been to Dunkirk in June 1940. But now, because the London County Council had paid for the new building in St John's Wood, the school was 'controlled' instead of 'aided', and a few years later that proved to be a change of immense significance.

While Collyer's was 'aided' and Quintin was 'controlled', King George V School, having been founded by the burgesses of the self-governing County Borough of Southport, was 'maintained'. It was a large and outstandingly successful grammar school, partly because in those days Southport was a large and outstandingly prosperous town. In 1949, when its first headmaster retired, after presiding over the school through twenty-nine years of development and growth, his place was taken by Geoffrey Dixon, who came from teaching at Uppingham before the war and from being Head of the Science Department at the Royal Military Academy, Sandhurst, after returning from military service in the Royal Corps of Signals, to lead the school through another twenty-seven years of stability and achievement.

Throughout those years Southport parents and the 11+ selection procedure provided the pupils, and the 11+ was still in place when I went there as headmaster in 1976. We had a hundred and twenty places to fill each year and the one hundred and twenty boys who got the highest average score in the three elements of the 11+ examination got the places. The level of ability required for that limited number of places was such that we could be sure that they would perform very well a few years later in public examinations.

Plenty of the other four-fifths of candidates would also have been capable of doing well, but they had 'failed' and were sent to a secondary modern school, unless their parents found the money to send them to one of the many private schools which sprang up locally to cater for 11+ failures. KGV, as the school was known locally, attracted able and dedicated men to serve on the staff and had a deservedly high reputation. As a 'maintained' grammar school its future was in the hands of the local education authority, and that authority was the County Borough of Southport, whose elected councillors were immensely proud of both King George V School and the Southport High School for Girls.

Collyer's, Quintin and KGV were just three among the 1,285 grammar schools which in 1965 were educating about a quarter of all those in secondary education. Former grammar school boys, and increasingly former grammar school girls as well, were helping to revitalise post-war Britain. More and more working-class children were staying on into the sixth form, and more than half of all Oxford and Cambridge scholarships were being won by boys and girls from grammar schools.

But whereas in the 1930s it had seemed wonderful that grammar schools provided free scholarship places for clever working-class boys and girls, now it increasingly seemed disgraceful that so few children had the benefit of a grammar school education and were condemned to go to a 'secondary modern'. It was a cause of great distress to many parents who would willingly have paid grammar school fees if they had been allowed to. They resented having their children told at the age of eleven that they were failures, and they did not want the next generation to be humiliated in that way.

The ruthless, inefficient and unpleasant 11+ examination system by which officials selected children for one type of education or another was not, of course, the fault of the grammar schools. It was the fault of a system over which they had no control. But increasingly they were blamed for it and resentment of the 11+ turned into resentment of the grammar schools. By abolishing fee-paying places in all except the independent and semi-independent 'direct grant' schools, the politicians gave themselves the comforting illusion that they were promoting equality. In practice they were doing the opposite. More and more parents who could afford it paid to send their children to independent schools, and by the 1960s many of those who could not afford to do so were demanding change.

The political and social case for getting rid of the 11+ examination was very strong, and as early as 1957 the Leicestershire local authority did away with it and sent all its children to middle schools, from which they could transfer to upper schools at fourteen. It was a particularly sensible development, though with the problem that the 1944 Act had fixed the age for moving from primary to secondary education at eleven, whereas ideally the change to a middle school would have been a couple of years earlier.

By the early 1960s many in the educational world were arguing for three stages of schooling, primary, middle and upper, and in a now long-forgotten Education Act of 1964, passed shortly before the Conservatives lost a general election, the then Minister of Education, Sir Edward Boyle, introduced a measure which allowed local authorities to cut across the distinction between primary and secondary education at eleven. It was a potentially good solution to the problem of secondary reorganisation, though to be really effective it need to be established throughout the country – if only because of the staffing problems thrown up by having different systems in different areas.

The growing public demand for comprehensive reorganisation was widely based on the assumption that there was a simple choice between either continuing with grammar and secondary modern schools or else having 'all-through' comprehensives covering the whole 11–18 age range. To those ideologically committed to comprehensive schools the middle school solution seemed to concede that comprehensive schools could not cover the whole 11–18 age range as effectively as grammar schools did, so in most of the large conurbations such as London and Manchester and Birmingham and Liverpool, where the local authority was committed to comprehensive reorganisation, the possibility of a three-tier system was ignored.

Providing a fairer education system and getting rid of the 11+ appeared to require the destruction of the grammar schools, which now suffered from the attitudes of politicians in both the main political parties. In the post-war years the Conservative Party was dominated by men educated at the major public schools (Churchill at Harrow, Eden and Macmillan at Eton, for example), and they viewed the country's grammar schools with little understanding and with that same patrician condescension that A.J.Balfour had shown when H.A.L.Fisher told him that he had accepted the Presidency of the Board of Education. Balfour 'raised his eyebrows and expressed misgiving that a man of ability should go to education'.

During the Second World War, when R.A.Butler was President of the Board of Education, Churchill described his job as 'wiping the children's noses and smacking their bottoms during wartime'. The leaders of the Labour Party were partly men similarly educated at public schools (Attlee at Haileybury, Dalton at Eton, Cripps at Winchester) and partly men like Ernest Bevin and Herbert Morrison who had been to elementary schools and saw grammar schools as devices for turning bright working-class boys and girls into middle-class Tory voters.

In the ancient world seafarers had had to navigate the treacherous waters of the Straits of Messina, avoiding running onto a rock, Scylla, on one side or being swallowed by a whirlpool, Charybdis, on the other. In the twentieth century English grammar schools had to navigate the treacherous waters of English politics. They were caught between the Scylla of Socialist suspicion and the Charybdis of Conservative contempt. Few survived unscathed. They had been among the most successful and most admired schools in the world, but in the storm of educational politics in the 1960s and 1970s they were scattered in all directions.

Many were submerged as parts of comprehensive schools in which the dominant element was often the 'sec-mods' with which they were combined. That happened to Quintin School. About a couple of hundred became independent schools, whether 'direct grant' grammar schools in the North, such as Manchester Grammar School and Merchant Taylors', Crosby, or 'voluntary aided' grammar schools in the South, such as Emanuel School in Wandsworth and Hampton Grammar School in Middlesex. More than another hundred became sixth form colleges. That happened to both Collyer's and King George V School. A few, such as St Marylebone Grammar School in central London, closed. Out of 1,285 in 1965 just 164 survived as grammar schools half a century later.

CHAPTER 8

Circular 10 of 1965

In 1964, after nearly half a century in which the grammar schools had grown in prestige and become important engines of social mobility, a former grammar school boy, Harold Wilson, became prime minister, and for the next thirty-three years all five prime ministers, two of them Labour, Harold Wilson and James Callaghan, and three of them Conservative, Edward Heath, Margaret Thatcher and John Major, were former grammar school pupils. Three, Wilson, Heath and Thatcher, went on to Oxford. Two, Callaghan and Major, left early to start work. As beneficiaries of a grammar school education none of them wanted to see those schools destroyed, but nevertheless it was during the thirty-three years of their premierships that most grammar schools were destroyed or transformed. The tide of the comprehensive movement was flowing strongly and none of them knew how to hold back the waves. Nor did any of them have a vision of how to create an integrated national system of secondary education.

Once the generation which had been humiliated by failing the 11+ had grown up, there was inevitably a demand for change, and there was widespread resentment that so few children were deemed suitable for grammar school education. Many middle-class parents resented not being able to choose a grammar school education for their children, especially when they would willingly have paid for it. Many working-class parents resented the inadequate opportunities for social mobility for their children. Resentment at the lack of sufficient grammar school places gradually turned into dislike of what came to be seen as the élitism of the grammar schools. Private schools flourished, and more and more were founded, to provide a relatively cheap but socially acceptable alternative to the 'sec-mod', and at the same time more and more people looked forward to an era when all children would be educated together in comprehensive schools.

Many of those who wanted comprehensive schools for all had a vision of an ideal educational future. It was one based on egalitarian theories, and Equality had become a more fashionable notion than Equality of Opportunity. Those who had once feared the power of the aristocracy now began to fear the potential power of a new meritocracy – and the grammar school was seen as a breeding ground of the meritocrat. Increasingly it was suggested that it was scandalous that grammar schools should be bastions of privilege for the clever. The advocates of comprehensive schools understandably saw themselves as seeking high quality education for all. But in practice the campaign to have comprehensive schools involved them in working to destroy high quality education in grammar schools, and unintentionally the outcome was to make high quality academic education more and more the preserve of the rich.

By 1965 nearly twenty years had gone by since the imposition of the 11+ examination throughout the country. Many local authorities wanted to get rid of it, and even before a Labour government was elected in 1964 ninety of them, more than half of the total of 169, already had plans drawn up for secondary reorganisation. When Anthony Crosland took over as Secretary of State in January 1965, they were already standing 'like greyhounds in the slips, straining upon the start'. He spent six months consulting with local authorities and teachers' organizations and then let loose the dogs of war, sending out his famous Circular 10/65 to all local education authorities requesting them to submit proposals for the reorganisation of secondary education on comprehensive lines.

Nearly ten years earlier, when he wrote *The Future of Socialism*, he had said that it would be absurd 'to close down the grammar schools, while leaving the public schools still holding their present commanding position. This would simply intensify the class cleavage by removing the middle tier which now spans the gulf between top and bottom'. But now he planned to do just that, and in paragraph 14 of Circular 10/65 it was made clear that what was wanted was 11–18 'all-through' comprehensives. If grammar schools could cope with that age range, it was to be assumed that comprehensive schools could do so as well.

That was a mistake. He failed to recognize the danger that the new comprehensive schools would be too big, with sixth forms that were too small. Dividing pupils up by age would have been a sensible approach, but for no good reason it was made clear that that would only be acceptable for a limited period. Instead local authorities were encouraged to plan for what was probably the worst form of reorganisation available: the all-through 11–18 comprehensive school.

As Secretary of State Crosland seems to have deliberately ignored the real problems, which were the unfairness of the 11+ examination, the lack of enough grammar school places, the lack of technical schools, the inappropriate curriculum in secondary modern schools, the lack of parental choice, and above all the division between the independent schools and those maintained by local authorities. Instead of tackling those problems, he led an attack on the grammar schools, which were the most impressive element in England's 'state' education system and an immense national asset.

His former colleague, Emanuel Shinwell, who had started work in 1894 at the age of eleven and was in his sixties when he served in the post-war Labour government from 1945 to 1951, had understood the issues better. In 1958 he wrote, 'We were afraid to tackle the public schools to which the wealthy people send their sons, but at the same time are ready to throw overboard the grammar schools which are for many working-class boys the stepping stone to the universities and a useful career'. He was right that it would have been very difficult for Labour to 'tackle the public schools', but at least he recognised the problem, while Crosland by 1965 seems to have deliberately missed the point and gone along with the developing public mood.

In 1967 Harold Wilson, whose own view was that every child should have a grammar school education, moved Crosland from the Education Department to the Board of Trade, but by then the damage was done. Ten years later Crosland suddenly and unexpectedly died, and in 1982 his widow, Susan Crosland, published a biography of him. In it she describes how he said to her, 'If it's the last thing I do, I'm going to destroy every fucking grammar school in England'. Educated at Highgate School, a minor public school in North London, and at Trinity College, Oxford, a college with a reputation for seeing itself as socially superior, his attitude to grammar schools was a particularly extreme example of that mixture of dislike, contempt and suspicion which was characteristic of many leading politicians of both major parties. Thus was Labour Party policy was formed. The Tories looked on not knowing what to do.

Anthony Crosland's circular provoked a vigorous and even bitter debate from which neither side emerged with credit. Few on either side did the necessary practical calculations, or, if they did, they could not be heard amid the clamour and anger and self-righteousness of the opposing parties. W. B. Yeats had famously said that 'the best lack all conviction; the worst are always full of passionate intensity'. That was vividly illustrated in the battle over comprehensive education. While the advocates of comprehensive schools preached the bright new comprehensive dawn, with the naive assumption that the creation of such schools would automatically result in better education and a more equal society, the defenders of grammar schools saw themselves as upholding academic standards against barbarians who, for reasons which had little to do with education, threatened to destroy not only the grammar schools but also much of what was most valuable in the British way of life.

Many people involved in education in other countries saw the destruction of their grammar schools by the English as extraordinary. An American, James Koerner, put it like this: 'Academically these schools must be among the best the world offers, and socially they are as mixed and democratic as thousands of schools in America or anywhere else. For the English people now to set about destroying their educational system seems to me, if I may put it candidly, sheer masochism. It is a triumph of political dogma over common sense'. A Hungarian Communist Party member, speaking in a wine cellar in Budapest, told Harry Judge, later Head of the Education Department at Oxford University and at the time Principal of Banbury Comprehensive School, that the whole comprehensive movement was a plot by the English ruling class to rob the workers of their free academic schools. It was an understandable viewpoint.

The arguments about comprehensive reorganisation seldom involved a realistic assessment of how schools work and usually ignored the important point about grammar schools that they were able to cope with the extraordinarily wide age range of eleven to eighteen because of the coherence of their educational provision. Children arriving at a grammar school at eleven were faced with prefects aged eighteen, who were already young men or women, preparing to take A level and go on to university. Most of the new boys, and increasingly girls as well, aspired to do the same themselves, and in a typical grammar school with an annual intake of a hundred and twenty, and thus six hundred in the five years to O level, there would be another two hundred and forty in the sixth form, which was seen as the crown and glory of the school.

Comprehensive schools found it far more difficult to cover that same 11–18 age range. In the 1960s they might need an intake of six hundred pupils a year and a total pre-O level pupil population of 3,000 to produce a sixth form of two hundred and forty. But a school of over 3,000 was seen as too big. It would be more sensible to have three schools of not much more than a thousand each. But then each of them would have an unworkable sixth form of only about eighty, and in practice, as numbers drained away to surviving grammar schools and independent schools, the number would be reduced to sixty, which was the average size of an English sixth form in the mid-1970s. Some had sixth forms of sixteen or six, and by then the sixth form was seen as irrelevant to the main business of the school, disproportionately using up scarce resources.

Furthermore, if one assumes a sixth form of sixty, with half of those sixty in the Lower Sixth and the other half in the Upper Sixth, and if each year is neatly divided into a Science and an Arts Sixth, each with fifteen pupils, a rational provision of sixth form education, in circumstances in which sixth formers generally took three A level subjects, would be a straight choice between an Arts course of English Literature, History and French or a Science course of Mathematics, Physics and Chemistry, with no other choice of subject. Very understandably most head teachers of comprehensive schools would not wish to provide so limited a range of A levels, but they would only be able to offer other options, such as Latin, German, Spanish, Geography, Further Mathematics, Biology and perhaps Economics and Geology, or even Law and Sociology, by shifting resources, most particularly of staffing, from the earlier years.

That is the reason why, before long, the sixth form came to be seen in some comprehensive schools as an offence, damaging to the education of the rest of the pupils, and why those who taught the sixth form could be seen as failing to contribute fully to the real work of the school. A choice had to be made between restricting the number of subjects offered at A level and spending a disproportionate amount of one's resources on small sixth form sets. There was no right answer. Most comprehensive schools settled for an unsatisfactory compromise.

These problems could be foreseen. There were others which emerged later, such as the difficulty some grammar school teachers faced when trying to cope with the bottom stream in the Fourth Form of a comprehensive school, or the difficulty some secondary modern teachers had in coping with bright former grammar school children. On the one hand, years of teaching Chaucer and Shakespeare to clever grammar school boys and girls was not necessarily a good qualification for seeking to establish and maintain order among fourteen-year-olds, while trying to ensure that they achieved a basic standard of literacy. On the other hand, a pass in O level Mathematics was an inadequate qualification for a former member of staff in a secondary modern school now trying to teach pupils who, under the old dispensation, would already have been studying A level Further Maths. But for the moment the obvious problems were enough.

Labour politicians generally felt that the principles of Equality and Equality of Opportunity bound them to encourage the development of comprehensive schools, even though those two principles are in direct conflict with each other, and even though some, such as Neil Kinnock, leader of the Labour Party from 1983 until 1992, regretted the loss of the grammar school which had transformed his life.

Most Conservative politicians also disliked the movement towards comprehensive schools, but, like Margaret Thatcher, Secretary of State for Education from 1970 until 1974, they simply watched helplessly. In 2013 the former Conservative cabinet minister, Michael Portillo, commented on television on the destruction of Harrow County School for Boys, where in 1964 he had won a scholarship to Cambridge, and said that 'it seemed stupid; it seemed like vandalism'. On the same programme another former Tory minister, Edwina Currie, who had been at school at the Liverpool Institute High School for Girls and won a scholarship to Oxford, said much the same. But when their party was in office neither they nor anyone else had been able to think of an acceptable alternative policy.

Chapter 9

The Inner London Education Authority

In 1965, the same year that Crosland's Circular 10 was published, the Inner London Education Authority, the I.L.E.A., was created to take responsibility for education in the twelve Inner London boroughs and the City of London. It immediately plunged into comprehensive reorganisation with more zeal than sense and set out to create comprehensive schools covering the age range 11–18 in a way which led to disaster in the immediate future and did immense and often irreparable damage to the education of a generation or more of young Londoners. It ended up with schools which were too big with sixth forms which were too small, and by the law of unintended consequences it helped to create an ever more unequal and divided society.

Because grammar schools had been able to educate boys and girls from the age of eleven to eighteen, it was mistakenly assumed that comprehensive schools would be able to do the same. That was a disastrous mistake. At a time when only a minority of the population went on to university comprehensive schools found it far more difficult to cover that same 11–18 age range, and it was particularly difficult for them to run a sixth form of a practicable size when there were so many public and private schools, as well as direct grant and voluntary aided grammar schools, which were willing and able to cream off the sixth form students – in the case of the direct grant grammar schools sometimes, and in the case of the voluntary aided grammar schools always, without charging any fees.

The I.L.E.A. was faced with the problem that its plans for a comprehensive system could not encompass most of the selective schools in the capital. It could not reorganise the independent schools, which had no representatives of the I.L.E.A. on their governing bodies. Nor could it reorganise the direct grant and voluntary aided grammar schools, on whose governing bodies there was only a minority of representatives of the I.L.E.A.

Those minorities were never going to be able to persuade their colleagues to vote for destroying the school for which they were responsible. What is more, as the I.L.E.A. merged the maintained and voluntary controlled grammar schools into its newly created comprehensive schools, the surviving independent, direct grant and voluntary aided schools were able to raise their entry standards as competition to get into them became more intense.

I had a front row view of how the I.L.E.A.'s policy affected Quintin School, because I was the Head of History there from 1960 until 1967. When I went there it was already voluntary controlled rather than aided, because in 1956 the former London County Council had provided the new building in St John's Wood, and thereafter the local authority had a majority on the governing body.

So long as the London County Council was the local education authority that made no difference, but it became immensely important in 1965 when the I.L.E.A. was formed and adopted its policy of comprehensive reorganisation of secondary education. Here was a good grammar school in the Borough of Westminster which it did have the power to reorganise.

Necessarily the problem for Quintin School as it faced comprehensive reorganisation was that so many selective secondary schools in the area from which it drew its pupils were able to continue unchanged. In the Inner London area there were leading public schools such as Westminster and St Paul's, other public schools such as Highgate and Mill Hill, two direct grant grammar schools, Alleyn's and Latymer Upper, three voluntary aided grammar schools, Emanuel, about five miles to the south, William Ellis in Hampstead, only two miles to the north-east, and St Marylebone, not much more than a mile to the south.

The I.L.E.A. could not turn any of them into comprehensive schools, because of its lack of control of their governing bodies. None of those governing bodies would for a moment contemplate having their school changed into a comprehensive, and the government made no attempt to change the law to enable the I.L.E.A. to do that.

What is more, less than three miles to the south-west of Quintin School was Holland Park Comprehensive, purpose-built in 1958 as the flagship of the comprehensive movement, 'the Socialist Eton', set down in the middle of an area which had the highest average house prices in the whole of England, and where Labour cabinet ministers could demonstrate their Socialist credentials by sending their children to a comprehensive school, and where for thirteen years Caroline Benn, wife of the Labour politician Tony Benn, was Chair of Governors.

Education officers of the I.L.E.A. visited Quintin School in 1966 and explained their plans to the staff. The intention was to create an 11–18 comprehensive school out of Quintin and the adjacent secondary modern school, Kynaston, which was named after Sir Kynaston Studd, who had succeeded Quintin Hogg as the second President of the Regent Street Polytechnic.

It was very quickly clear that, coming at the end of a pecking order of independent schools, direct grant grammar schools, voluntary aided grammar schools and a purpose-built and fashionable comprehensive school, the proposed Quintin Kynaston School would in practice be a very large secondary modern school under another name. The ideological decision took little or no account of the practical problems likely to result from it.

No doubt the local politicians of the I.L.E.A. and their education officers were frustrated by the legal framework within which they had to operate, but even within that framework they could have made more sensible arrangements. Kynaston School had a natural connection with Quintin School, and it might have made sense to make it a Junior High

School, covering the age range eleven to fourteen, and to have made Quintin a Senior High School doing O and A level courses.

But to pretend that the combination of the two of them was a comprehensive school at a time when there were so many independent and surviving grammar schools nearby was to plunge it into a disaster from which it would take decades to recover – if, indeed, it ever did. It also resulted in years of unsatisfactory schooling for hundreds of teenagers, and one could not help but suspect that something similar was the fate of hundreds of other teenagers in inner-city comprehensive schools all over the country.

I was the first of the heads of department to leave – in 1967. From a personal point of view it was a good time to move. It was my seventh year there and during that time all three of our children had been born and a book I had written on modern history had just been published. I applied for the post of Head of History at Stowe School near Buckingham and was appointed. Over the next eighteen months five other heads of department left: the Head of English for an independent Roman Catholic monastic school, the Head of Modern Languages to a lectureship at Glasgow University, the Heads of Mathematics and Biology to posts in university education departments, and the Head of Physics to a Canadian independent school.

Thus six heads of department were lost, not just to Quintin School but to the 'state' sector of education – three to independent schools and three to universities. By September 1968, the beginning of Quintin School's last academic year before officially becoming Quintin Kynaston School, all six had gone. The three other heads of major departments, Classics, Geography and Chemistry, were all nearing retirement and stayed to cope as best they could.

When I visited the school to see old friends a year after reorganisation, I saw as I walked up to the main entrance that the rose beds on either side had been trampled down. Just inside the main entrance on the right was a door which led to the school office and the headmaster's study. It was locked. The library was boarded up. There was graffiti on the walls and there were surly-looking boys in the corridors. It was entirely unlike the school I had left a couple of years earlier.

Rather extraordinarily Kynaston and Quintin boys continued to wear their distinctively different uniforms and Kynaston boys jeered at 'Quintin queers' in their green blazers with red trimmings, while Quintin boys hit back at the 'Kynaston cunts', using language not significantly worse than that of the Secretary of State who had helped to put them in this position. It was a sad change from the school I remembered.

The headmaster, who had managed well as the head of a good grammar school and had the administrative skills needed to manage the reorganisation of Quintin and Kynaston as one school, was never going to be able to deal satisfactorily with the human problems which would inevitably face him. Nevertheless, he was appointed as the first head of what was theoretically a comprehensive school and struggled on for five years with ever increasing problems until in 1972 he had a nervous breakdown and had to retire early. At about the same time his deputy had a heart attack and died.

Many years later, when I walked past Quintin Kynaston, now usually known as QK, on the way to visit a friend who lived in St John's Wood, I saw that the whole site had been enclosed within a tall metal barrier – as if a prisoner-of-war camp had been set down in the middle of the expensive and exclusive residential area of St John's Wood. Whether it was to keep the pupils in or everyone else out was not clear.

My successor as Head of History, Michael Barcroft, came from Gordonstoun, where he had been teaching Prince Charles. He took over for the summer term of 1967, stayed three more years and left in 1970 to be the headmaster of a school in Peterborough. So the post of Head of History was once again advertised.

This time one of the applicants was a former pupil of mine from my first year at Quintin. David Akers had left in 1961 to go up to Cambridge to read History, got a Football Blue as well as his history degree and in 1965 started teaching at the Brighton, Hove and Sussex Boys' Grammar School. By 1970 he was well qualified for the post of Head of History at his old school and was invited for interview.

Many years later, when we were both retired and sitting in my garden having lunch, he told me how John Price, the Head of Classics, with whom I had shared the coaching of the school VIIIs on the river, had taken hold of him as he walked down the corridor, pulled him into a side room and asked him what he was doing. John Price warned David of the danger to his future career if he accepted the post, so he returned to Brighton, where the grammar school became a sixth form college a few years later. He became the Head of History and stayed there until he retired.

A new headmaster, Peter Mitchell, took over at Quintin Kynaston in 1972, by which time things could scarcely have been worse, and stayed for eleven years. Failing schools do not need a super-head to come in for a year, 'turn things round' with a lot of money and a lot of noise, and then move on elsewhere. They need someone who will stay long enough to live with the consequences of his (or her) own decisions. Peter Mitchell did that, and under him the school began to recover. In 1976 it started to admit girls, and he stayed until 1983.

He and many members of staff worked hard to make QK a good school, but no amount of effort and idealism, and there was plenty of both, could entirely overcome the problem that it was only theoretically a comprehensive school and was situated in a part of London where those living in the immediate vicinity were, even in the days when Quintin had been a good grammar school with high academic standards, more likely to go to Westminster or to Stowe or to Clifton than to the grammar school just over the road. I taught more boys from that immediate area when I was at Clifton before I went to Quintin, and more at Stowe after I left, than I ever taught while there.

Many boys at Quintin School travelled very considerable distances in order to go there, but the chances of anyone from the immensely prosperous immediate vicinity attending the school had always been slim. Comprehensive reorganisation made the problem significantly worse. No amount of hard work and idealism could overcome the problem of the difference between leading independent schools and comprehensive schools. Many expensive independent schools clearly had increasingly high academic standards. Meanwhile, publicly funded comprehensive schools equally clearly had depressingly low academic standards by comparison with the grammar schools they had replaced.

Not only did the I.L.E.A. end up with schools which were too big with sixth forms which were too small. It also helped to create an ever more unequal and divided society. Whereas the difference between the public schools and the grammar schools had been blurred at the beginning of the century but had become an understandable cause for concern by the 1940s, now the significant dividing line in English secondary education was between on the one hand the selective schools, both the public schools and the surviving grammar schools, and on the other hand the ideologically admirable but in practice academically weak and sometimes ill-disciplined comprehensive schools.

As for the I.L.E.A., it continued with even more ideological fervour after an internal Labour Party coup in 1981 shifted power into the hands of a hard left group. It was anathema to the Conservatives, who were by then in government, and under the terms of what was called the Education Reform Act of 1988 it was abolished with effect from 1990. From then on all the various inner London boroughs became education authorities, each responsible for trying to improve the standards of the comprehensive schools it had inherited.

CHAPTER 10

From Comprehensives to Sixth Form Colleges

In 1965, a year in which someone said that there were now only two sorts of school, comprehensive and apprehensive, there were still 1,285 grammar schools in England and Wales. Little more than ten years later there were only 477 left, and many of them, including King George V School, Southport, where I took over as headmaster in 1976, were due to undergo substantial change of one sort or another. As the number of grammar schools declined, the number of comprehensives increased. In 1965 there had only been 262. By 1976 there were 2,878 and three-quarters of all children of secondary age were attending them.

Most of that change happened while Margaret Thatcher was Secretary of State for Education and Science. Edward Heath appointed her in 1970, thinking that he ought to have a woman in his cabinet and that a post at Education was a suitable job for a woman. She had no policy of her own, other than to tell the local education authorities that they were no longer expected to submit plans for comprehensive reorganisation.

But the tide of the comprehensive movement was flowing strongly and plans for comprehensive reorganisation continued to come in. She disliked it but had no idea what to do about it and so, lacking a policy of her own, she approved more plans for comprehensive reorganisation than any Secretary of State before or since. In 1970, when she took office, the proportion of children of secondary school age attending comprehensive schools was less than a third. By the time she left office in 1974 it was nearly two-thirds.

Other than that there were only two changes of any significance during her time as Secretary of State. One was the decision in 1971 to withdraw the provision of free school milk, as a result of which she was remembered as 'Margaret Thatcher, Milk Snatcher'. The other was the raising of the school leaving age to sixteen with effect from September 1972.

Much the same problems arose as had arisen after the raising of the school leaving age to fifteen back in 1947. In many parts of the country comprehensive schools were provided with prefabricated 'mobile' buildings named after the Raising of the School Leaving Age, and the ludicrous situation developed that, in many of these schools for which there had been such high hopes, teenagers, bitterly resentful at having to remain at school for an extra year, were trapped in the specially provided ROSLA blocks.

There was even more resentment and unrest than when the leaving age had been raised to fifteen, and it never seemed to occur to anyone in authority that the teenagers were right to object to the way they were being treated, and that some serious thought needed to be given to providing a form of education which they would value and which would be of some use to them, instead of simply improving the unemployment figures by increasing school numbers.

Even as Margaret Thatcher approved more and more plans for reorganisation, the failings of the comprehensive schools were becoming ever more obvious. Particularly in inner city schools there were problems with discipline, with mixed ability classes, and with small inadequate sixth forms. Of course the money put into schools, the hard work of thousands of teachers, and some careful planning and effective leadership often had good outcomes, but in too much of England the very word 'comprehensive' came to sound like a term of abuse.

Discontent was at its height in predominantly Labour areas, because that was where many of the worst comprehensive schools were to be found. Fewer and fewer bright working-class boys and girls had the opportunity to have the sort of education they would have had a generation earlier, and it was not for want of dedicated teachers. The teachers as much as the pupils were trapped in a profoundly unsound system – though of course it was not a system, but rather a variety of different arrangements arising from idealism mixed with ignorance.

The Conservatives gave no thought to developing a plan for an integrated national system. Tory politicians knew that 'people like us' sent their children to independent schools where they did not have to mix with the masses, and they had little interest in making plans for schools to which other people sent their children. Many of them resented grammar schools, secondary moderns and comprehensive schools alike as institutions to which they would not send their own children but for which they nevertheless had to pay their taxes.

They also tended to be contemptuous of grammar school boys and girls who went up to university with the serious-minded intention of working hard and doing well in their examinations, knowing that they had to rely on their own ability rather than their parents' connections or the old school tie to get them a job afterwards.

Labour politicians similarly had no plan for an integrated national system, let alone one which would embrace the public schools. They left local authorities to adopt a variety of different arrangements and seemed to believe that the gradual extension of the comprehensive ideal would somehow solve not only all educational problems but all social problems as well. They ignored the existence of the public schools as if the problem would go away once the comprehensive Utopia was attained. They attacked the grammar schools as dangerously élitist, as if there was something wrong with academic excellence. They entirely ignored the point that it was not the grammar schools but politicians who had insisted on the disastrous 11+ selection procedure.

Ever since the public schools and the grammar schools had both existed, there had always been a social gap between them. That gap became wider after 1944, when it became illegal for most grammar schools to charge fees. Then, as the grammar schools were destroyed and replaced by comprehensive schools, the gap between the public schools and the mass of schools maintained out of the public purse became a chasm. The merit of comprehensive schools was intended to be above all that all children would be educated together. They were not, and Conservative and Labour politicians alike, rather than face that problem, complained about what was going wrong, blamed the local education authorities and the teachers, and talked about the need to drive up standards.

The most obvious structural problem with 11–18 comprehensive schools was that they were too large, with sixth forms that were too small. That was sometimes dealt with effectively. In the town of Banbury in Oxfordshire, for example, a comprehensive school of about two and a half thousand was developed from 1967 onwards under the headship of Harry Judge, formerly the headmaster of the grammar school and later the Director of the University of Oxford Department of Educational Studies. It was divided into three 'Halls', which operated as more or less separate schools for the first four years of secondary education, after which all the pupils transferred to an Upper School. Each of them, the three Halls and the Upper School, had its own head, while Harry Judge co-ordinated the operation and presided over it as Principal.

Then, shortly after a new Labour government had come to power in 1974 and local government reorganisation had brought Oxford itself within the jurisdiction of the Oxfordshire local authority, 'middle schools' were established in the town for the years 9–13, so that the comprehensive schools had a limited age range of 13–18. Cherwell School in North Oxford flourished under the headship of Martin Roberts from 1981 until 2002, partly because it had that limited age range, partly because it was in what can be described as a 'good' catchment area, and despite being in competition with several independent schools no more than five miles away: Radley and Abingdon catering for boys, the Oxford High School and Headington for girls, and St Edward's and Magdalen College School for both.

Not just in Oxfordshire but throughout the country local authority education officers were coming to realise that if children were not going to be divided by ability, then it was necessary to divide them by age. In Banbury the change was made at fifteen, in Oxford at thirteen; my own preference would be fourteen. But in much of England it was seen as convenient to make the change of school at sixteen, simply because after 1972 that was the school leaving age. The consequence was the development of sixth form colleges.

There was no great sixth form college movement such as the comprehensive movement, but already in the 1960s a few colleges had been started as a practical expedient, more were created in the 1970s and even more in the 1980s, so that by the 1990s there were about a hundred and twenty of them, educating roughly a quarter of all the country's A level candidates.

Some saw this as an effective way of extending the comprehensive principle into the 16–19 age range, while others welcomed it as a way of having 'grammar schools at sixteen plus'. Whichever way one looked at it, it was a rational solution to the problems thrown up by the comprehensive movement. Instead of a town having a number of 11–18 comprehensive schools, each of them too big and with a sixth form that was too small, it was possible to have comprehensive schools covering the age range 11–16 and just one sixth form college for all those who wished to continue their education beyond the age of compulsory schooling. It was an effective way of providing high quality education for large numbers of young people aged 16–18.

The change of King George V School in Southport into King George V College provides a good example of how and why a grammar school changed into a sixth form college. The self-governing County Borough of Southport in Lancashire had held out against secondary reorganisation throughout the decade following Circular 10/65. But local government reorganisation in 1974 put Southport, together with Bootle, Crosby and Formby, into the new Metropolitan Borough of Sefton in Merseyside, and the new local education authority was faced with the problem that KGV needed rebuilding.

The school suffered from the problem that it was built on peat. Most of Southport was built on a sand bar between the estuaries of the rivers Ribble and Mersey, and despite the warning in St Matthew's gospel, sand had proved to be a firm foundation. But there was a problem when one moved a couple of miles inland, where began the area of peat left over from what had once been the largest inland lake in England, and the peat on which King George V School was built was a significantly less good foundation than sand.

Over fifty years the school had gradually subsided into the ground until in the 1970s it clearly needed to be rebuilt. The Department of Education would not approve the rebuilding of a grammar school, so the new council had to face some form of comprehensive reorganisation. Fortunately, enough was known by then about the problems of 11–18 comprehensive schools in Liverpool that it was decided that Southport should have 11–16 comprehensive schools, with KGV as a sixth form college.

The headmaster, Geoffrey Dixon, who had for the previous decade fought a rear-guard action against reorganisation, also played an important part in ensuring that reorganisation, if it was unavoidable, would be carried out in a manner which made sense. Then, once the decision was made, he decided that sixty-three was an appropriate age at which to retire and let a new headmaster preside over the transformation of the boys' grammar school into a sixth form college which would also embrace the town's sixth form girls.

I arrived to take over from him at the beginning of the academic year which started in the autumn of 1976, with the great advantage that my previous career at Clifton, Quintin School and Stowe was entirely in schools with high academic standards, for the councillors had decided that KGV was to be an academic college providing traditional A level subjects and the sort of sports and recreational activities traditionally associated with a grammar school. 'We don't want students coming here to take courses in origami and belly-dancing', said one of the governors, 'They can do that at the Tech'.

The reorganisation of secondary education in the whole town was largely in the capable hands of Mike Nichol, the local authority's Deputy Director of Education, and he ensured that we were able to appoint a well-qualified and experienced staff admirably suited to the teaching and care of students in an academic sixth form college.

Less satisfactory were the arrangements for rebuilding, for the least impressive element in the Education Department of the Metropolitan Borough of Sefton was its Buildings Branch. It got hold of specifications from the Department of Education for a replacement boys' school, copied them and started to build the college with no girls' toilets and with the designs for classrooms and laboratories as if for a boys' comprehensive school.

The problems were eventually resolved at the cost of untold hours of argument and explanation, and we ended up not only with a curriculum well suited to our students and a first-rate staff, but also with new, well-equipped buildings in which teaching and learning could flourish. The new college had an ethos in which the encouragement of purposeful activity was combined with unobtrusive but effective supervision, good teaching, careful guidance about higher education, and a generally amiable atmosphere. It was a model of 'a grammar school at sixteen plus'.

Sixth form colleges had a number of substantial advantages over schools. Not only were there obvious efficiencies of scale, but they also attracted well-qualified, specialist staff. In a world in which the tenure of academic posts in universities was precarious, some young men and women would opt for a career teaching A level students, when they would not consider joining the staff of even a good grammar school in which they would have to teach the whole age range from eleven to eighteen. Under those circumstances KGV and many other sixth form colleges flourished. There appeared to be a possibility that England was bit by bit moving towards a system of comprehensive education which would work not only in theory but also in practice.

CHAPTER **11**

The Direct Grant and Voluntary Aided Schools

In 1976, the year in which I went as headmaster to King George V School, the Labour government which had come to power in 1974 put in hand the measures it had determined on the previous year to drive the surviving grammar schools into the comprehensive system. For the previous decade the direct grant and voluntary aided grammar schools, with a majority of foundation rather than local authority representatives on their governing bodies, had been able to avoid becoming comprehensive schools. But now the Labour government devised ways to put pressure on them to become comprehensives.

In the case of the direct grant schools it decided to withdraw the direct grant which had been provided for the past half century in return for free places for clever working-class children. Almost all the schools with which King George V School had for years competed at cricket and rugby football, and also at trying to get the largest number of open awards to Oxbridge, were direct grant grammar schools. The grammar schools in Blackburn, Bolton and Bury had all existed since the sixteenth century, Merchant Taylors' School down the coast in Crosby had been founded in 1620 by a member of the Merchant Taylors' Company, Arnold School in Blackpool, on the other side of the Ribble estuary, had been founded in 1896 and named after Dr Arnold, the headmaster of Rugby School, and King Edward VII School, Lytham, had been founded in 1908 by the Lytham Charity Foundation.

Since 1926 each of them had received a direct grant from the government in return for providing a percentage of free places, and in accordance with the arrangements established under the terms of the

1944 Education Act they all took a mixture of fee-paying pupils and others who received free places on the strength of a good performance in the 11+ examination. Now they were faced with the withdrawal of the direct grant as financial pressure was exerted to make them become comprehensive schools. There was a total of nearly two hundred such schools in the country, most for boys, some for girls and a few mixed.

There was not one of them whose governors would have wanted the school to educate only the children of the wealthy, nor did any of them want full independence such as was enjoyed by the public schools. They prided themselves that their schools were engines of social mobility. But they also saw themselves as existing to educate children with 'some aptness for learning', from whatever social background they might come. They were concerned to maintain high academic standards, parental choice, a wide social mix, as many free places as possible and a sliding scale of payments according to income for the rest. That view of things was not reconcilable with a determination to 'end selection'.

Political dogma triumphed over common sense and the government gambled that the direct grant schools would not have the financial strength to carry on as grammar schools without the direct grant to support them. It was a serious miscalculation. Schools such as Manchester Grammar School, Bradford Grammar School, the Royal Grammar School, Newcastle upon Tyne, or Bristol Grammar School, many of them far older and with far higher academic standards than most public schools, were not going to vote for their own destruction. They decided to become independent, and as an inevitable consequence they had to raise the money previously provided by the direct grant by raising their fees.

Overwhelmingly the direct grant schools chose independence rather than be turned into what a Labour prime minister later referred to as 'a bog-standard comprehensive'. A Labour government had managed at the stroke of a pen to create more than a hundred new independent boys' schools, as well as a large number of independent girls' schools. Since the former direct grant schools were only able to make up for the loss of the direct grant by charging higher fees and reducing the number of free places, the opportunities for talented children from poor backgrounds to go to a school with high academic standards and a broad range of other activities were fewer than they had been for decades. The politicians had achieved the opposite of their declared intention. The gap between the independent schools and what were often misleadingly called 'state' schools became wider.

This happened at a time when there was much concern among the middle classes about the trade unions demanding higher pay and better working conditions for their members. Two things about that went largely unnoticed. The first was that pay demands were usually expressed in percentage terms, so that a 10% pay rise meant an increase of only £100 to someone earning £1,000, while it meant an increase of £10,000 to someone on £100,000. The second thing which for many years was scarcely commented on in the press was that, while most employees in a business might get a 10% pay rise, the senior executives would get a 50% increase, and their pay would go up from £100,000 to £200,000. The gap between the rich and the poor was getting ever wider.

Those who could be counted as rich needed to find the money to pay the ever increasing fees of independent schools, sometimes for two or three children at a time, the cost of private health insurance, a mortgage on a second home and the cost of running at least two cars.

There had been a time when some Socialists had looked forward to a time when everyone would live in houses built and owned by a local authority, use gas, electricity and water provided by their local municipality, travel on cheap or even free public transport, be cared for by a National Health Service and a national insurance system, and send their children to state schools.

Many Conservatives, by contrast, had looked forward to extending affluence, so that most people could own their own home, buy gas, electricity, water and anything else they wanted from private companies, drive their own car, consult private doctors, arrange their own insurance and send their children to independent schools.

By the last quarter of the twentieth century both Labour and Conservative politicians had exchanged those ideals for a common belief in a mixed economy. At one extreme of society were the very rich who lived on inherited wealth, travelled by private jet and sent their children to expensive independent schools, while at the other extreme were those of the poor who lived on 'benefits' and unwillingly sent their children to 'state' schools.

Most people lived somewhere between those two extremes. Gradations of class and social status were complicated, but they could be very important for a child's life chances, and one of the clearest declarations of class and social status was the school a person attended.

Government policy also had a damaging effect on recruitment of academically well qualified graduates into the teaching profession. It was at some time in the mid-1970s that the Admissions Tutor of a Cambridge college told me that he had been teaching Geography there for the last twenty years or so and each year had another new group of about half a dozen undergraduates to teach. During the first few years in his time at the college, in the 1950s, more than half of them usually went into teaching, at universities, grammar schools and public schools. In the last few years only two of them had gone into teaching – both at independent schools. It was one of the unintended consequences of comprehensive reorganization that the prospect of years of teaching a very wide range of ability over a similarly wide age range made a career in teaching less attractive than it had been in the past to many Oxbridge graduates. Most now went into the City and made a lot of money.

At the same time as the Labour government withdrew the direct grant from the direct grant grammar schools, it required the voluntary aided grammar schools to enter into discussions with their local education authorities about how they could best be integrated within the comprehensive system. That was almost as big a miscalculation as the withdrawal of the direct grant, because the voluntary aided grammar schools also had a majority of foundation governors on their governing bodies and it would only be in very particular circumstances that they would decide on anything other than independence.

The main exception to this was the Roman Catholic voluntary aided grammar schools. The hierarchy of the Roman Catholic Church decided to keep their grammar schools within the maintained sector and the governing bodies of twenty of them negotiated with their local education authorities to become sixth form colleges. Four other voluntary aided grammar schools did the same: Ludlow, an ancient endowed school founded in about 1200, Collyer's in Horsham, founded in the reign of Henry VIII, King Edward VI, Stourbridge, and King Edward VI, Nuneaton.

The complications of the way in which reorganisation came about in English secondary education can be illustrated by an example from West Sussex. When local authorities were requested by Anthony Crosland's Circular 10/65 to consider plans for secondary reorganisation of education on comprehensive lines, the West Sussex County Council and its Director of Education did as they were asked and over the next decade dismantled most of their grammar and secondary modern schools and replaced them with comprehensives – though rather peculiarly they still called some of them grammar schools.

But they had no power to compel a voluntary aided school to change its admissions policy, and the governors of Collyer's had no intention of admitting boys of a wide range of ability to their grammar school. So in 1966 the local authority's recommendation for Horsham was 'that for the time being the Horsham schools continue on the present basis'.

Ten years later the Labour government legislated to require the governing bodies of voluntary aided grammar schools to enter into discussions about joining the comprehensive system, gambling that they would not be able to survive without public funding. Most declined to accept any proposal for comprehensive reorganisation, and their local authority could do nothing other than submit a proposal to the government for ceasing to maintain the school.

It was nearly as bad a misjudgement as the withdrawal of the direct grant. The overwhelming majority of voluntary aided grammar schools became independent. There were four no great distance from Collyer's. Reigate Grammar School, about fifteen miles to the north-east of Horsham, and the Royal Grammar School, Guildford, about twenty miles to the north-west, were both in Surrey. Shoreham Grammar School, a similar distance to the south, was in West Sussex. Churcher's in Petersfield, about thirty miles to the west, was in Hampshire. All became independent schools.

Meanwhile, however, the West Sussex Director of Education, Roy Potter, came up with a scheme which enabled him to persuade the representatives of the Mercers' Company, who dominated the Governing Body of Collyer's, to reach agreement with the West Sussex Education Authority. He pointed out that under existing legislation, while the governors were responsible for providing the buildings, the local authority was responsible for providing a specified area of playing fields. As it happens, because Collyer's had its own grounds, the County Council had never provided it with any playing fields. So to remedy this the County Council would pay £218,000 for four acres of the school's land and then give the land back to Collyer's, thus fulfilling its obligation to provide a playing field area.

The money would enable the governors to undertake a substantial building programme, since under the recently modified terms of the voluntary aided agreement central government would have to pay 85% of the cost of new buildings, the Governing Body of Collyer's

15%, and West Sussex nothing. For the moment £45,000 was needed to provide 15% of the total cost of £300,000 for a new classroom block. The remaining £173,000 could go into a 'Collyer Endowment' maintained by the Mercers' Company along with its other investments, and be used to provide 15% of subsequent building projects.

Collyer's would change from being a voluntary aided boys' grammar school into a voluntary aided mixed sixth form college and would have a substantial building programme to provide all the extensions and adaptations which would be necessary in order to provide adequately for all the sixth form students in the area. The Horsham High School for Girls and the secondary modern schools in the town would become 11–16 comprehensive schools.

Roy Potter had saved the West Sussex County Council the millions of pounds it would have cost if Collyer's, like most voluntary aided grammar schools, had become independent and the local authority had needed to spend millions on a new school or college in Horsham. Instead they had acquired a sixth form college at the relatively trivial cost of the £218,000 paid for an area of playing field which was returned to the college to fulfil the local authority's obligations under the voluntary aided arrangements. Eighty-five percent of all future expenditure on the college's buildings would be paid by central government and not by West Sussex.

The advantage to Collyer's was that it got at least the first phase of new sixth form college buildings, with some promise for the future, as well as the money with which to pay its 15% of that future expenditure. The advantage to West Sussex was that it would not have to pay anything towards future buildings. The advantage to the Mercers' Company was that Collyer's brought money with it instead of costing it money at a time when the company was involved in spending many millions of pounds on its schools.

At just that time it was rebuilding St Paul's Boys' School at Barnes and moving the St Paul's Girls' School into the Hammersmith buildings which had previously housed the boys' school. Next it was engaged in the substantial rebuilding and refurbishment of Abingdon School in Oxfordshire and of Dauntsey's in Wiltshire. Both of them had been founded by members of the Mercers' Company and both were direct grant grammar schools. Now that the direct grant was being withdrawn and they were becoming independent, they needed considerable resources put into them as they rebranded themselves as ancient public schools.

CHAPTER 12

The Independent Sector

In 1961, in a book called *The Conservative Enemy*, Anthony Crosland had written about the public schools that it was necessary 'to assimilate them into the state sector ... democratise their entry' and limit 'the power of the rich to buy social privilege through buying private education'. It was, he asserted, necessary to have 'either a radical reform or none at all'. But when he became Secretary of State for Education in 1965 he found it easier to attack the grammar schools. Although in Circular 7/65 he set up the Public Schools Commission 'to advise on the best way of integrating the public schools with the state system', he later acknowledged that his civil servants were right to point out that nothing it recommended was going to be acceptable on either financial or political grounds.

Although the public schools and grammar schools were both engaged in educating teenagers up to the age of eighteen, the tone or ethos of the public schools was very different from that of the grammar schools. I recall my first staff meeting at Stowe in April of 1967, the day before the Summer Term began, when, after I had been welcomed as a new member of staff, the next item on the agenda was an explanation of the precautions to protect the school beagle pack from the outbreak of foot and mouth disease in the countryside over which it was accustomed to hunt. The third item on the agenda was about how far it was acceptable for boys to keep shotguns in their studies when they had been given permission to shoot over a neighbouring farmer's land. I do not remember the outcome of the discussions in those far-off days before Health and Safety Legislation would have decided the issue unequivocally, but I do remember thinking that I had come to a very different environment from that to which I had been accustomed in a London grammar school.

By then the traditional public school ethos was far less generally admired than half a century earlier and the very term 'public school' had acquired a flavour of social snobbery which was distasteful not only at large but even within the schools themselves. It was already becoming increasingly usual for members of staff in such schools to speak of them as 'independent schools', either deliberately or sometimes unconsciously avoiding the term 'public school'.

The idea of independence from government control was altogether more acceptable than an image of fagging, beating, cold baths, tackling low and playing a straight bat, all of which was associated in the public mind with 'public schools' and was no longer as acceptable as it had once been. Then in the late 1970s, when the Labour government drove so many 'direct grant' and 'voluntary aided' grammar schools into the independent sector, the word 'independent' was very convenient as a label embracing both the public schools and a large number of grammar schools.

The period from 1970 until 1974, when Margaret Thatcher was Secretary of State, saw an expansion of both the comprehensive system and the independent sector, and the Conservative government which came to power under her in 1979 was happy to accept the way in which the Labour government of 1974–79 had further boosted the independent sector. The development work going on at Abingdon and Dauntsey's in the late 1970s and early 80s was similar to that going on in most of the former direct grant and voluntary aided grammar schools all over the country as they adjusted to their new status as independent schools.

Back at the beginning of the twentieth century there had been only eighty-nine public schools in England and Wales. Now the heads of more than three times that many were members of the Headmasters' and Headmistresses' Conference, which represented the leading independent schools in England and Wales. Most of those schools had become independent as the unintended consequence of pressure by a Labour government to turn them into comprehensives.

The independent sector now included former direct grant schools such as Manchester Grammar School and Bristol Grammar School and former voluntary aided schools such as Hampton Grammar School and the Royal Grammar School, Guildford. Like so many others, they had opted for independence rather than become comprehensives, and the arrival of a large number of grammar schools in the independent sector produced a significant change.

Back in the nineteenth century, when the public schools had generally been admired, small endowed grammar schools such as Sherborne and Uppingham were proud to have changed into public schools and preferred to forget their grammar school past. Their standing rested less on academic excellence than on social exclusiveness, and they built a reputation for educating 'the whole man' and preparing their pupils for positions of leadership both at home and throughout the empire. Now that the ideal of the public school was less generally admired, the public schools gradually became rather more like grammar schools, while the grammar schools became more like public schools.

At one end of a very wide spectrum were the most famous of the public schools, starting with Eton, Harrow and Winchester. At the other end of the spectrum there were schools such as Manchester Grammar School, still proud to be known as grammar schools. In the middle of the spectrum the distinction was blurred. Abingdon and Dauntsey's, Merchant Taylors', Crosby, and Emanuel School were simply independent schools.

The former public schools had gained in academic respectability and many of them were now concerned as never before with improving the quality of their teaching and learning, raising the level at which they would admit pupils and improving their examination results.

At the same time the former direct grant grammar schools in the industrial north and many former voluntary aided grammar schools in the south gained greater social respectability among those who judged a person's social status by the schools their children went to. As 'independent schools' they were now obviously both socially and academically acceptable by comparison with the local 'comp.', and the word 'independent' increasingly suggested the academic success which followed on from selective entrance arrangements, good teaching and high standards of dress and behaviour. By implication all these things were not usually to be found in the maintained sector.

The significant dividing line in English secondary education was now between the independent schools and the mass of 'state' schools, with all that implied of bureaucratic inefficiency, indiscipline, scruffy appearance and low standards. The politicians had gone one stage further towards creating a situation in which the rich paid for their children to go to independent schools, whose standards were rising, while those on low or middle incomes had to put up with what their local authority provided, which too often, especially in the inner cities, was something with which they were dissatisfied.

The only significant education policy in the early years of the Conservative government which took office in 1979 was the introduction and promotion of an Assisted Places Scheme to help middle-class children who did well in the entrance examination for an independent school to escape from their local comprehensive. At that time many independent schools were flourishing, but as and when they got involved with either local or central government, the arrangements which they agreed could not be relied on to last. Politicians changed; so did policies. Even independent schools could be bruised by political decisions made both centrally and locally.

For nearly four hundred years Christ's Hospital had been untouched by central or local government. Then for about twenty years after the 1944 Education Act was implemented in 1947 London boys and girls who did particularly well in the 11+ examination and whose parents had a low income were offered a place at Christ's Hospital. Many took it. But the creation of the Inner London Education Authority in 1965, with its zeal for comprehensive education, deprived the next generation of that opportunity. The hospital, of course, had to adjust to the change of policy, but for many years the average level of academic ability of its intake was lower than when it had had a regular intake of bright working-class London children.

Clifton College, founded more than three hundred years later than either Collyer's or Christ's Hospital, was one of that large number of public schools which came into existence in the middle of the nineteenth century. From its foundation in 1862, and for more than a century thereafter, it remained independent of any involvement with either central government or its local education authority and rose to be recognised as one of the great public schools of the country. Then in 1980 Margaret Thatcher's government introduced the Assisted Places Scheme, under which the government was prepared to pay about four times as much money per pupil as the amount spent on children in the state sector.

Clifton, which had always had day boy houses ever since it was founded, was the first school in the country to join the Assisted Places Scheme, so the first pupils funded by the scheme entered the school in 1981. It became a regular feature of the school's admissions policy, but in 1997, when Tony Blair became prime minister at the head of a new Labour government after eighteen years of Tory rule, the scheme was abolished. Clifton had to adjust and returned to complete independence.

One inevitable consequence of that withdrawal of financial assistance was that it pushed Clifton's fees higher, but the school was well enough established that that was not a significant problem and in the early twenty-first century it was one of the small group of leading public schools able to charge fees of over £30,000.

Stowe, though the most recently founded of all six of the schools where I spent fifty years of my life, always remained entirely independent of both local and central government. It had its own difficulties. After J.F. Roxburgh retired in 1949, neither of his successors could match the esteem in which he had been held and both retired early in their mid-fifties. But then Stowe acquired another outstanding headmaster, R.Q.Drayson, who presided over the school during the sixteen years from 1964 until 1979 while the comprehensive revolution was taking place in the state sector.

He took the opportunity to appoint a number of relatively young new heads of department, many of them from grammar schools. Shortly before me arrived Peter Longhurst as Head of Economics from King George V School in Southport and David Manly as Head of Modern Languages from the grammar school in Abingdon. Then I arrived from Quintin School just three years after Bob Drayson in 1967 and left three years before him in 1976.

The ethos of Stowe was relaxed and attractive and had something of the atmosphere of a country club set down in what the architectural historian, Sir Nicholas Pevsner, described as 'the most perfect combination of architecture and landscape gardening in the country'. But the world was changing, and during the years I was there I was consciously engaged, together with a number of my colleagues, in seeking to improve academic standards.

Over the next thirty to forty years Stowe was increasingly able to compete successfully in terms of its academic performance with the leading boarding schools in the country, and in 2014, when it opened its new Music School costing £7,000,000, it was having no difficulty in attracting pupils whose parents could pay more than £30,000 a year. It had recently built two new girls' boarding houses and was planning to spend a similar amount, perhaps twice the annual funding of a typical sixth form college, on extending and improving the Science Building.

Schools such as Stowe and Clifton were able to flourish despite charging high fees. Indeed, the fact that their fees were so high tended to confirm the impression that they were good schools. But in the twenty-first century fees of over £30,000 a year were coming to be a concern to many parents whose background was such that they had expected to educate their children privately but could no longer pay to do so out of taxed income.

In May 2012 a freelance journalist, Stephen Robinson, an old boy of Westminster School, wrote in *The Spectator* of his worries about the education of his own children: 'Like many of my privately educated friends, I find I spend a humiliating amount of my day pondering my family's educational downward mobility. Neil Kinnock famously made much of the fact that he was the first Kinnock in history to have gone to a university. I am haunted by the fear that our little darlings will be the first Robinsons since the repeal of the Corn Laws to go to a bog-standard secondary school, where they won't be taught about *Magna Carta*, but will learn how to put a condom on a banana'.

He pointed out that since the early 1980s fees in the leading public schools had trebled in real terms, detaching them from their natural constituency, the middle classes, and causing them to seek their pupils from investment bankers, Russian oligarchs, German businessmen, the Chinese new rich and those with either a family trust or substantial inherited wealth. By then, in 2012, the fees for a day boy at St Paul's were nearly £20,000, and, meanwhile, Robinson's old school, Westminster, with boarding fees of over £30,000, was asking its former pupils to contribute towards raising a sum of forty-six million pounds for a new sports centre in the middle of London.

Going to an independent school was no guarantee of learning about *Magna Carta*. Although the prime minister at the time, David Cameron, had been to Eton and Oxford, he was unable to translate the words *Magna Carta* when appearing on an American chat show. But Stephen Robinson was right that fees at the leading independent schools were now, at over £30,000, so high that many of those people who in the nineteenth century would naturally have sent their sons to a public school (local tradesmen, solicitors, clergy, officers in the armed forces and civil servants) could no longer do so out of earned income. Meanwhile, many of them were unhappy with what was provided by their local education authority and assumed that, if they could not afford independent education, their children would be at a disadvantage later in life. They were not necessarily wrong.

CHAPTER **13**

The Examinations System

Both the grammar schools and the public schools made use of the examinations system set up when the Secondary Schools Examinations Council was formed in the middle of the First World War in 1917. The council introduced the School Certificate, aimed at pupils aged sixteen, who were required to pass examinations in English Language, Mathematics, a foreign language and at least two other subjects in order to get a certificate. It also introduced the Higher School Certificate, aimed at those who stayed at school until they were eighteen. To acquire a Higher Certificate it was necessary to pass in at least two main subjects and a subsidiary subject. The idea was that a relatively broad academic curriculum up to the age of sixteen would be followed by specialisation during the next two years in preparation for university.

Those arrangements continued until, after the implementation of the Butler Education Act in 1947, it seemed necessary to change the system to take account of increasing numbers of academically weaker candidates. In 1951 Ordinary, or O, Level replaced the School Certificate and Advanced, or A, Level replaced Higher Certificate. It was now no longer necessary to get a specified number of passes. Both examinations could be passed in just one subject, and the fact that one was either illiterate or lacking any understanding of simple arithmetic was no obstacle to acquiring a certificate in whatever subject one could manage to pass.

Over the years the system of marking was changed to increase both the percentage of those passing and the percentage of high grades, until eventually universities found it difficult to discriminate between all the many candidates with A grades (not just A level, but A grade at A level, as distinct from the B, C, D and E grades, which were also pass grades), and many employers found much the same when seeking to employ members of staff. They complained that something was wrong. It was.

The problem was more complicated than was widely realised. For example, as more girls stayed on at school to take School Certificate, then Higher Certificate, and then go on to university, employers complained of lower standards. At one time their secretary had been able to could correct their grammar and spelling and write their letters for them. That was no longer so. Girls who would once have been glad to have a job as a secretary were now going to university and on to careers as lawyers, doctors, civil servants and businesswomen, while girls who in the 1930s would have been cleaners or shop assistants were now secretaries.

The explanation for what appeared to be a lowering of standards was paradoxically that standards generally were improving. The problem with English secondary education was not that standards overall were lower, but rather that the social and academic divide between independent schools and the rest was widening. Year after year the independent schools became less 'comprehensive' academically than they had been, as they moved towards admitting only pupils who could be expected to do well in examinations.

Where once they would have been happy to recommend a pupil to an Oxford or Cambridge college on the strength of his parental background, his admirable qualities as a school prefect and his performance on the cricket field, that was no longer possible, and they were now concerned that the school's average performance at A level should be seen to be impressive. Where members of staff would once have taken some pride in teaching a weak candidate well enough that he or she scraped a couple of bare passes, now the school was anxious to admit only those who would get at least three high grades.

If they made a mistake and admitted an academically weak pupil into the sixth form, they could avoid damage to their average results by requiring him to enter the examinations as a private candidate. It was not a change for the better.

When most of the direct grant and voluntary aided grammar schools became independent, the academic gulf between independent schools and most of the maintained sector became so wide that an examination system originally designed with grammar schools in mind was now only suitable for the independent sector. The mass of comprehensive schools needed something less taxing.

At first those who went to secondary modern schools did not usually take any examination, but eventually a new examination for academically weaker candidates, the Certificate of Secondary Education, was devised with pass grades from 1–5. It was first taken in 1965 and a grade 1 at CSE was deemed, at least theoretically, to be the equivalent of an O level pass. That produced the problem that, while a CSE grade 1 was deemed to be the equivalent of an O level pass, the grade was not specified, and there was the further problem that the syllabuses of the courses leading up to the O level and CSE examinations were so different that pupils with a CSE grade 1 who wanted to go on to take A levels could find that they had to spend the next year getting the qualifications which theoretically they already had.

That is only one of many practical problems thrown up by the changing arrangements for secondary education. Teachers had to decide which pupils should take courses leading to O level and which should take courses leading to CSE. The problems were considerable. Should a pupil take O level in some subjects and CSE in others? How far should decisions be influenced by the numbers in the various teaching groups? The scope for misjudgments and disagreements was vast, and comprehensive schools were sometimes faced with the demand, though seldom from anyone with any experience of teaching, that all children of a given age should be taught together regardless of ability. Even with that there is the complication that it can work reasonably well with a subject such as History or Geography but is disastrous with Mathematics or Latin. That in turn has practical implications which are clear to anyone who has ever had to make a school timetable.

Understandably there came to be a demand for one examination for everyone. So in 1988 O level and CSE were replaced by GCSE (the General Certificate of Secondary Education). Further pass grades of D, E, F and G were devised to take account of weaker candidates, but they were pass grades only in theory. In practice employers who had previously asked applicants for a job for a given number of O level passes now asked for GCSE passes at Grade C or above. Large numbers of teenagers now not only had to endure a low-level academic curriculum entirely unsuited to their needs; they also knew that their school years were doomed to culminate in examination results which would generally be regarded as failure.

That soon led to the argument that the whole way examinations were conducted was inappropriate for pupils who did not do well in examinations but could work well on their own, especially if they could take their own time over a task. The proposed solution was to count an element of course work as a significant part of the material on which a candidate's performance at GCSE was judged. As a way of assessing some practical competence, such as how well a student could make a table or cut someone's hair, that made sense, so long as there was sufficient supervision to ensure that it was the student's own work. Applied to academic work undertaken by a student at home it was ludicrous. Nevertheless it came to be an accepted part of GCSE level examinations.

It was never quite clear where the line should be drawn between having a conversation with one's parents or a sibling about a course topic and having all the work done by them. So the system favoured those with an older brother or sister at university, or with well-educated parents who could help with the course work or even do the whole thing. A pupil without those advantages might have no help at all and also difficult conditions in which to work at home. The balance of advantage was shifted unnecessarily, improperly, though also unintentionally, against the poor. No wonder that the proportion of children from working-class backgrounds going on to Higher Education was declining rather than rising! Not only had they been deprived of their grammar schools. Now they also had the examination system stacked against them.

The next shift in the examination system proclaimed as a reform went unnoticed by most of the general public. It involved a change from what in educational jargon was called 'norm-referenced' results to 'criterion-referenced' results. There used to be approximate percentages for the various O level and A level grades. Candidates who did outstandingly well would get a grade A, which indicated that they were in roughly the top 10% of those taking the examination. A similar number of those who performed poorly would fail. There was a sense in which it was a competitive examination which enabled university admissions tutors and employers to know who was in the top 10% or 25% or 50% in any year. That was seen as objectionable by those who wanted every candidate to be able to achieve a high grade. They wanted teachers and pupils to be told in advance what the criteria were for achieving a particular grade, and then all who subsequently met those criteria could get that grade – however many they were.

Again, as a system for assessing whether or not someone should pass a driving test or be graded for their performance on a musical instrument, that made sense. As a way of assessing performance in an academic examination it was a serious mistake. It put pressure on teachers to tell their pupils what were seen to be the 'right' answers, it led to multiple choice questions and to a quarter of a century in which the number of high grades in examinations increased year after year, as politicians congratulated themselves on driving up standards, while the general public understandably talked of 'grade inflation' and declining standards.

Since compulsory schooling did not continue beyond sixteen in the later years of the twentieth century, the demand to modify A level examinations to take account of candidates with a low level of academic ability took longer than the demand for change at O level. After all, those staying on into the sixth form were all volunteers, or at least had been volunteered by their parents. But as more and more young people stayed on, and as more and more were encouraged to apply to university, change at that level was demanded as well and before long there was talk of grade inflation and declining standards with A level as much as with GCSE. In 1976 about 70% of those taking A level had got at least one pass. By 2014 it was 96%. The first time any pupil I taught ever got 100% on an A level History paper was after I had retired but had undertaken to teach medieval history one evening a week to an adult education class. One of my pupils got all the answers 'right'.

By the twenty-first century, with competition seen in political circles as the key to success in all areas of human activity, the examination boards were competing with each other for customers by making it easier for candidates to get high grades. They were publishing books with answers to examination questions matching the criteria for high grades. They were running expensive 'conferences' at which they would give advance information about the coming examinations to the representatives of the schools which had paid to attend. They even sold model answers to the questions. It caused no more than a mild scandal. In a world in which members of parliament were routinely fiddling their expense accounts and investment bankers were gambling with other people's money, losing it and paying themselves vast bonuses for doing so, it perhaps seemed no more than a minor peccadillo. I saw as a serious offence and was surprised that it did not result in prosecutions and prison sentences.

From 1992, when a Conservative government required the publication of every secondary school's examination results, those results were increasingly the measure by which both independent and maintained schools were judged. Each year national and local newspapers published schools' average GCSE and A level results in the manner prescribed by the government. Everywhere selective schools came out top, and those which excluded weaker candidates at sixteen, and others after a poor performance in trial examinations, came out at the very top. Political pressure from both left and right had required most schools and colleges maintained out of the public purse to have a 'comprehensive' intake, but now the politicians required the publication of examination results in a manner which proclaimed the superiority of schools with a selective intake.

A good example of a school which regularly year after year proclaims its academic success publicly is Brighton College. It is a very successful independent school with high standards for entry into the school, into the sixth form and into A level examinations and each year it claims to have the best results in Sussex. Its average results are indeed the best of all the independent schools in Sussex, and local newspapers, in line with the government's policy of applauding success and shaming low levels of achievement, print pictures each year of attractive-looking, rich and clever pupils at Brighton College, wearing smart uniforms and waving their results with joy.

As it happens the number of A level results achieved each year by the sixth form college in the centre of Brighton is always higher than the number achieved at Brighton College. The same is true of the number of A grades. But that is not what is published. What the government requires is the publication of average results, and any selective school which avoids having to educate academically weaker students necessarily has better average results than a college which educates teenagers across the whole range of ability. The same applies all over the country. Published examination results, as required by the government, have become a way of proclaiming the superiority of selective schools over any with a comprehensive intake.

CHAPTER 14

'Economy, Efficiency and Effectiveness'

In the early years of the Conservative government which came to office in 1979 little was done about education other than the setting up of the Assisted Places Scheme. Meanwhile, British industry was increasingly critical of English schools. As employers looked for a qualified workforce they saw too many school leavers as ill-disciplined, illiterate and scarcely numerate, and in May 1986 the prime minister, Margaret Thatcher, appointed Kenneth Baker as Secretary of State for Education and told him to 'work up some ideas'.

Baker had begun his secondary education at King George V School, Southport, during the Second World War and completed it after moving to London at Hampton Grammar School and then at St Paul's. So at least he had direct personal experience of something other than a public boarding school, and he had three main aims. One was to establish a national curriculum, so that children could move from one part of the country to another and have some continuity in their education. The second was to establish technical schools to provide the sort of education that teenagers would value. The third was to arrange for the devolution of secondary schools' budgets from local education authorities to the individual schools.

Each of those aims was admirable, but when the government sought to give effect to them by means of the Education Reform Act of 1988, the manner of its implementation had unfortunate consequences. First, the national curriculum was set up in such a way that it placed too much power over detail in the hands of the Secretary of State, with potential for trouble in the future. Secondly, the new City Technology

Colleges were not so much technical schools as comprehensive schools with computers, and there were only ever fifteen of them, each funded centrally and kept under the direct control of the Secretary of State, so that instead of being part of a national system administered locally, they were a few free-standing schools controlled centrally. The third and most successful of the main changes introduced in the 1988 Act was the devolution of budgets to schools, but that was done in such a way that it appeared to be an expression of the government's dislike of and distrust of local government.

It was a matter of faith among Conservative politicians at that time that anything run privately was always going to be better than the same thing in the public sector. So there was a vigorous government policy of privatisation – of the railways, of the iron and steel industry, and of the provision of gas, water and electricity, with different companies competing to maximise profits for their shareholders while providing a service which the consumer would choose. There were plans for privatising prisons and hospitals in the hope that they would be run more efficiently, and one could not help but wonder if some members of the government thought that competing private armies, navies and air forces would provide more effectively for the defence of the realm.

At the same time Tory ministers assumed that spending on public services was always likely to be profligate and that the solution was central control in order to be able to reduce the funds made available, and thus produce the 'economy, efficiency and effectiveness' to which they were strongly committed. So rather peculiarly a belief in privatisation was combined with centralisation, and local authorities, set up by a Conservative administration a hundred years earlier, were now seen as an obstacle to the drive for reform.

Meanwhile, sixth form colleges were flourishing – so much so that many young people were leaving independent schools at sixteen to go to their local college. In the first four years after King George V School became a sixth form college in 1979 it admitted sixty-eight boys from independent schools, including Harrow and Rugby, Dauntsey's and Rossall, Ampleforth and Stoneyhurst, Millfield and Stowe, and a similar influx of girls from less well known independent schools.

Furthermore, the numbers joining from independent schools were steadily increasing. In 1979, the first year that KGV was a sixth form college, and shortly after the withdrawal of the direct grant had made Merchant Taylors', Crosby, independent, only two boys came from Merchant Taylors'. Four years later there were ten. During the 1980s the head teachers and the governing bodies of independent schools had good reason to worry about the success and popularity of the leading sixth form colleges. They were academically successful and they cost parents nothing. Just as there had once been an opportunity for grammar schools to compete successfully with the best independent schools, now there was an opportunity for sixth form colleges to do so.

It was a serious problem for the independent schools, but it was largely solved for them by the Conservative government led by John Major. In 1992, when the Conservative Party won a fourth election in a row, now under his leadership, it was committed to cutting taxes and reducing public expenditure, and the government's approach to education in the public sector was that it could be improved by emulating business. A reduction of funding and staff numbers would generate efficiency, and that in turn would lead to greater effectiveness. In particular the government believed that many technical colleges were using disproportionate resources for too little return, so they decided to take control of them away from local education authorities, set up a Further Education Funding Council, and impose financial rigour on a new post-sixteen education sector. All colleges in the sector would operate independently but be funded centrally.

They were right about the problem. Neglect of high quality technical education was endemic in England. As early as the sixteenth century the French philosopher, Montaigne, had suggested that a wise man should assess the value of anything he studied 'by its usefulness and appropriateness to his life'. But those who controlled English education had usually been educated in the humanities and seemed to find it impossible to get their minds round the idea that education should be both useful and appropriate to the lives of the students. Even now they were not making provision for technical education for those in their early teens, but only for those who had reached the school leaving age of sixteen.

Furthermore, and perhaps in order to give what could be seen as intellectual respectability to this new sector, they decided to include all the sixth form colleges (there were now about a hundred and twenty of them) alongside five hundred or more technical colleges, even though the work of the sixth form colleges in providing A level courses was entirely different from the work of the technical colleges. It was a mistake comparable with Labour's withdrawal of the direct grant and its pressure on the voluntary aided grammar schools in 1976.

First, by setting up the new Further Education Sector in 1992 the government ensured that no local authority would ever again create a sixth form college, because, as soon as it did, the college would be transferred to the post-sixteen sector. Secondly, the Further Education Funding Council consulted with all its colleges over the distribution of funding, accepted the advice of the technical colleges that funding for vocational courses should be increased at the expense of A levels, and distributed the available funds in such a way that a number of large technical colleges were able to take over smaller and financially weaker sixth form colleges.

Not only had the spread of sixth form colleges been abruptly halted; about a quarter of those which existed were destroyed. The rapid rise in the number of sixth form colleges in the 1970s and 1980s to about a hundred and twenty was followed by a reduction to no more than about ninety. Those which did survive did so despite ever decreasing funding to a level significantly lower than that of sixth forms in schools.

The government's intention was to cut the cost of educating

16 to 19-year-olds, while at the same time increasing student participation and driving up standards. It assumed that a reduction in funding would lead to greater efficiency and make possible the improvement and expansion of education at 16+, but by the law of unintended consequences it destroyed the one development, the rise of the sixth form college, which was promising to provide a national solution to the problems generated by comprehensive reorganisation.

In 1992 all principals of sixth form colleges were summoned to a conference to hear Jonathan Eggar, the Minister of State with responsibility for Further and Higher Education, speak about the government's intentions. It had, he explained, won the election earlier that year with a promise to cut taxes, and it was now going to make those tax cuts possible by slashing public expenditure. In the case of post-16 colleges it would reduce the total funding for the coming year by 5% and any pay rises would have to come out of further 'efficiency gains'. In practice, since pay at that stage was determined by a national agreement covering all teachers, that meant a further 3% reduction in funding, or 8% overall.

He went on to say that by removing us from the stultifying control which up till then had been exercised by local authorities, the government was freeing us to use those entrepreneurial skills which were essential for the chief executive of any organisation such as one of our colleges. He was confident that we would rise to the challenge. 'After all', he finished, 'You wouldn't want the wheels to come off first in your own college, would you?'

The most obvious way to avoid substantial job losses was to recruit more students – something which fitted with the government's aim of reducing unemployment by widening participation in education for young people in the 16–18 age range. If a typical college recruited an extra 8% of students but employed no more staff and coped with the extra numbers by increasing the average taught group size, then, roughly speaking, that would make up for the 8% cut.

But an increased number of students could produce the problem that a college's buildings were inadequate to accommodate them. So one principal asked if the drive to increase participation was going to be matched by a government-funded building programme. Jonathan Eggar had clearly expected the question. 'No, certainly not!' was his answer. 'Most colleges can accommodate extra students in the rooms you already have. If you can't, then you can use those entrepreneurial skills I was speaking about to develop your buildings'.

He went on to give examples which stuck in my memory because of their relevance to what we had already done at Collyer's. 'You could make use of the undercroft of some buildings' (I had already done that with the college hall). 'You could put in a mezzanine floor' (I had done that in the Technology Block). 'You could convert a garage to teaching space' (I had done that to provide a photographic studio and darkroom). If you lack the necessary skills', he went on, 'you probably shouldn't be running a business like this and should make way for someone else'.

The FEFC was not a friendly organisation. Its officers aimed to micromanage the sector centrally and use financial pressure to get what they wanted. They sent out one circular after another with detailed instructions about what they would and would not fund, so that before long the job of a principal came to be largely a matter of responding to the requirements of the FEFC, while seeking to protect one's colleagues from accumulating bureaucracy, so that they could get on with teaching.

At an annual conference one principal pointed out the danger that FEFC policies were likely to cause his college to close. 'Then' came the answer in the distinctive Scottish accent of the Chief Executive, Sir William Stubbs, 'that would be some surplus stock taken out of the sector'. Another principal commented on the lack of funding for all the various activities which went to make up the ethos of a good sixth form college. 'I will not give you one penny for your ethos' was the answer from the FEFC's Finance Director. It was all very 'robust' and I reflected on what excellent *apparatchiki* the officers of the FEFC would have made in the People's Republics of Eastern Europe.

At Collyer's we were able to reduce the impact of the new funding regime in the first year of the FEFC by taking an extra sixty students, but no more staff, and as a result we had a more or less standstill budget. A year later one of the successive Ministers of State for Further and Higher Education, who seemed to come and go every few months either to a new job or to 'spend more time with their families', spoke to another meeting of sixth form college principals. The message was that, as we had managed the cuts during the first year of the new regime, we should be able to do it again. There would be another cut of 5%, and again pay rises would come out of further 'efficiency gains'. Centralisation was achieving what the government wanted.

The funding regime ensured that those sixth form colleges which did survive did so by making large scale economies. Funding was driven down to about a quarter of the level of independent day school fees and to about an eighth of the level of fees of the leading independent boarding schools, and survival was only possible with a significant reduction in pay expenditure. During the years I was at Collyer's, from 1983 until 1999, student numbers doubled from about six hundred to about 1,200, while the staffing level stayed at sixty. The student teacher ratio changed from 10:1 to 20:1.

That, of course, could be seen as a justification of the government's policy, since in financial terms the college was twice as 'efficient' as it had once been. But by that standard all independent schools could be regarded as seriously inefficient. Nevertheless, the best of them were having no difficulty in attracting pupils, and the damage done to sixth form colleges by annual reductions in funding was removing the danger of large numbers of independent school pupils leaving to go to their local college.

CHAPTER 15

The Curriculum

As early as 1964 a Tory Minister of Education, Sir Edward Boyle, set up the Schools Council to consider the curriculum and give advice on its development. Its members included local authority education officers, officials of the Department of Education and of the inspectorate, representatives of employers, of universities and above all of the teachers' unions and the various subject associations – anyone with an interest in what was taught in schools. It had no power and little influence and after twenty years of talking was abolished by another Minister of Education (or rather by now Secretary of State for Education and Science), Sir Keith Joseph.

During those twenty years I was much interested in curricular issues. For seven of them, from the late 1960s until 1976 I was the Chairman of the Stowe School Curriculum Committee, and for the next seven was responsible for the curriculum of King George V School, Southport, as a grammar school and then of King George V College as it became a sixth form college. Those were the days when the job description of a headmaster was simple and straightforward. He was responsible for the curriculum of the school and for the organisation and discipline of the staff and pupils. Other than that, it was assumed that he would not have been appointed unless he knew what to do.

I always took the view that the curriculum was the totality of the learning experiences which we deliberately provided, and my conscious aim was to pass on to our pupils those ideas and skills which we judged to be of value, assist them in developing their potential for good (academic, personal and social), help broaden their understanding, and provide them with qualifications to enable them to progress further. Just what pupils studied was heavily influenced by the examinations they needed to take and by decisions made by head teachers.

Thus, for example, as the headmaster of a boys' grammar school, I required all the pupils to take eight O level subjects, including English Language and French, Maths, Physics and Chemistry, and two other subjects chosen from among Latin, German, Music, History and Biology. The aim was to maximize the choices available to them when choosing what to study for A level. It was a practical decision, heavily influenced by past practice and by the examination system, but also underpinned by what I judged to be a high quality academic education.

As for the Schools Council, I scarcely knew that it existed but was interested in the sort of topics it discussed. Should schools aim to provide high quality specialised education or try to ensure a broad and balanced education for all? Should they emphasise academic or vocational education? Should teachers be more concerned with preparing their pupils for life or with providing them with useful qualifications? With all these matters I took the view that, although it was healthy to ask questions of that sort, the best answer was usually much the same as that given by Winnie-the-Pooh, wisest of bears, when Rabbit asked him if he would like honey or condensed milk with his bread. 'Both', Pooh had said, and then, so as not to seem greedy, he added, 'But don't bother about the bread, please'. That is, on all these issues there was something of value on both sides. There can be specialisation within a broad curriculum, 'academic' and 'vocational' can be complementary, and it should be possible to acquire useful qualifications while also being well educated. But it is also important to clear away the stodgy rubbish.

As the head of a sixth form college I came to realise that two serious problems had developed in English sixth form education by the late twentieth century. One was overspecialisation. The English sixth form curriculum was far more specialised than in other countries, and that specialised curriculum had been a remarkably successful preparation for university in the days when grammar school pupils had a broad academic curriculum up to O level. A level Mathematicians knew some Latin and some History, an A level languages specialist would have passed O level Maths and Physics, and politicians could take pride in England having outstandingly high standards.

But as more and more students of less ability stayed on in the sixth form, the level of specialisation was increasingly a problem. Students of languages or the humanities were going up to university with scarcely any mathematical or scientific understanding; some students of mathematical and scientific subjects were going up illiterate.

Paradoxically the second problem was that the range of subjects which students could choose to study at 'A' level was too wide. Politicians, the funding council and the inspectorate insisted that students should be given a free choice of a wide range of courses. But the requirement that there should be a wide range of courses available at A level is as misguided as the insistence on specialisation. Many subjects currently studied in English sixth forms would be better left until university. Economics, Sociology, Psychology, Law and Geology are examples. Others are better taught as part of the general education which should be provided for all. Computer literacy and the ability to make use of information technology are essential practical skills needed by all. Media Studies, which is disliked by many politicians because it encourages a critical approach to political speeches, newspapers, television, radio and advertising, is also valuable for all, but does not need to be a specialist A level subject.

What is needed in an academic sixth form is not only some specialist knowledge, but also a broad education, so that all those who leave at eighteen are literate and numerate and have some knowledge of the humanities, of science and of languages. Within that broad educational framework there is still scope for choice and specialisation, but by the late twentieth century it was going to be necessary to make some substantial changes to ensure that.

The government was not concerned that the curriculum was too narrow. On the contrary, the specialisation characteristic of English education remained a matter of pride. It also encouraged, and through the Further Education Funding Council even required, a wide range of subjects from which students could choose – and the efficiencies of scale which a sixth form college provided made it possible to offer a very wide range of subjects indeed.

But then, every summer when the A level examination results were published, the same politicians who demanded that students should be free to choose from a wide range of subjects could be heard voicing the complaint that too many were taking what they saw as 'soft' subjects, such as Sociology, Psychology, Law or Media Studies, when they should be taking 'hard' subjects such as Mathematics, Physics, Latin or a Modern Language. 'Something' should be done about it – anything other than reform the system!

Another problem with A level was that it was too difficult for some of the 'new sixth formers' who, despite a poor performance at O and later GCSE level, were now encouraged to stay on after the age of sixteen. They needed careful attention and tuition, and they needed to work hard if they were to achieve some success. But in many schools they were given too little to do and were left alone for too much of the week. A student who had not managed to get a grade C in either Maths or English at GCSE the previous summer might understandably be given no more than two A level subjects to do in the first year of the sixth form course, because of needing to concentrate on getting at least grade C passes in GCSE Maths and English. But such a student who then got those passes at the end of the first sixth form year might, meanwhile, have found one of the two A level subjects too difficult and given it up, and would then spend the second A level year doing just one subject badly and learning habits of indolence.

I was one among many head teachers and principals who thought that we needed a quite different post-16 curriculum, requiring all students to study six subjects: English, Maths, a science subject, a modern foreign language, a humanities subject and one more subject which could either be a second one from any of those five categories (Further Maths, for example, or a second language, or a second science subject) or else one of a limited number of other subjects, such as Music or Latin. Other elements in every sixth former's course would be computer literacy and critical thinking, as well as a choice of recreational activities. Some subjects such as Economics, Sociology, Law and Geology, which were quite widely taught in sixth forms in the late twentieth century, would in future not be taught until university.

Ideally it would be possible to take any or all of the subjects at either a higher or a lower level. Most students would probably study three subjects at the higher level, and three at the lower level. But it is possible to imagine a quite outstandingly gifted student studying Maths, Further Maths and Physics, English Literature, French and History, all at the higher level, while an academically weak student might study six subjects at the lower level.

In the mid-1990s something very like this was agreed by the college principals who formed APVIC, the Association of Principals of VIth Form Colleges. Although there were only a hundred and twenty of us, we were responsible for a quarter of all the A level candidates in the country. The proposal was also agreed by HMC, originally the Head Masters' Conference and now the body representing both the headmasters and the headmistresses of the leading independent schools. They were responsible for fewer A level candidates, but they had many who produced good results, because, of course, most of them were highly selective schools which in some cases accepted into the sixth form only those students who were clearly going to get high grades. Finally, the proposal was accepted by SHA, the Secondary Heads Association, representing those head teachers responsible for the mass of A level candidates in comprehensive schools, and also those in the few surviving grammar schools still maintained by local education authorities.

With APVIC, HMC and SHA united, there appeared to be a good prospect for fundamental reform of the post-16 curriculum. But the government was quick to dismiss the proposal. A level was 'the gold standard'. It was admired throughout the world. The government, concerned as it was for excellence, was not going to allow 'educationists' (a highly pejorative word in political language) to divert it from its task of driving up standards – a task in which it claimed to be succeeding, since the arrangements for assessing A level performance had changed so much that almost all candidates taking it now passed and a very high proportion got the top grade. So the double problem of having overspecialisation and having it in subjects chosen from an excessively wide range continued, while at the same time such a large number of students now got three or four A grades that it was difficult for universities to select the best candidates for admission.

Some independent schools moved away from A levels towards entering their best candidates either for the International Baccalaureate, which was similar to the recommendation the government had turned down, or for a new examination called the Cambridge Pre-U, designed to enable the leading universities to choose the best candidates. That choice was limited to candidates from a number of independent schools. Sixth form college students could not take the Cambridge Pre-U, because the Funding Council's funding 'methodology' did not provide for it.

At a political level the issue of the relationship between the independent and the maintained sectors was still ignored. Conservative politicians were content to leave things as they were. After all, they usually sent their own children to independent schools, and Oliver Letwin, a cabinet minister in the Tory government which took office in 2015, was on record as having said that he would rather 'go out on the street and beg' than send his children to a state school in London.

Labour politicians would from time to time complain about the independent sector, but many of them would send their own children to independent schools if they could afford it. Meanwhile, as the independent schools competed with each other to demonstrate their excellence by pushing their fees up faster than the rate of inflation and faster than each other, funding was cut further in the maintained sector, and particularly in the post-sixteen sector, where there was a continuing requirement for 'efficiency gains'.

The reason that the colleges in the post-sixteen sector were particularly singled out for funding reductions was that the government believed that most of them were sufficiently large that their size should make them cost-effective. Ministers appeared to take the view that, if supermarkets could flourish by stacking shelves with goods and selling them cheap, then colleges would improve if only they adopted the principle, 'Pile 'em in; teach 'em cheap'. The ideal was that colleges should survive by enrolling ever more students, who would be taught for as little time as possible, in groups as large as possible, by well-qualified, specialist teachers working long hours and paid less than primary and secondary school teachers – though perhaps more than university lecturers.

Meanwhile, financial pressure had the effect of pushing the sixth form colleges further and further in the direction of providing vocational courses which would have been better left to technical colleges. There continued to be a lack of high quality technical education for those below the age of sixteen, and the academic curriculum for those over that age remained unsatisfactory because of the obstinate failure of politicians to face the consequences of changes they had themselves brought about.

CHAPTER 16

Inspection, Auditing and Micromanagement

For half a century after the passing of the 1944 Education Act arguments about secondary education centred on the way schools were structured. The issuing of Circular 10/65 was followed by the restructuring of secondary schools all over the country on comprehensive lines. Legislation was passed in 1975 to get rid of direct grant and voluntary aided grammar schools and in 1992 to remove technical colleges and sixth form colleges from local authority control into a new post-16 sector. Then the fashionable opinion among politicians changed. Somehow they came round to the view that it was not the way things were structured that mattered after all. What mattered was 'standards', and politicians of all parties began to chant the mantra, 'standards not structures'.

The idea that England could have an integrated system of secondary education, as proposed by the Taunton Commission back in 1868 and recommended in the Fleming Report of 1944, was ignored. The solution was to accept things as they were and set up inspection systems to force indolent teachers and incompetent head teachers to drive up standards. It was as if they had agreed that it did not matter how an army was organised so long as every regiment could produce a training policy and every soldier was regularly inspected to check that he had shiny boots.

At a summer conference of all the principals in the Further Education sector the Chief Inspector spoke of simple arithmetical approaches which principals could use to improve things, and he held up King George V College in Southport as a shining example of a good college which did just that. As it happens it was there, as Headmaster, that I had many years before introduced the very systems he was commending, and I was pleased to hear that they were still in use twenty years later.

One was a grading system running from 1 to 5 as a way of judging students' academic performance as excellent (1), good (2), satisfactory (3), poor (4) and disastrous (5). The Funding Council had adopted precisely that scale for its inspectorate to use when judging anything from 'Governance' to 'Quality Assurance' – though the language used to describe each of the grades was far more convoluted than that.

Another was the practice of comparing the average A level performance of a college's top 50 or 100 students with the performance of leading schools. I had done that ever since league tables of A level scores were first published, and a couple of years before had written to the *West Sussex County Times* to make the point that Westminster, St Paul's, Eton and Winchester were all very good, very selective and very expensive schools, and were the only schools in the country whose average A level score was marginally better than that of the top 50 Collyer's students (i.e. 30.1, or a bit better than AAA), and only 18 schools in the United Kingdom produced an average A level score higher than that of the top 100 Collyer's students (26 or ABB). Each was expensive and highly selective, and five of them had only 70 or 80 candidates.

Shortly before that John Rae, the Headmaster of Westminster, had upset many of his fellow heads in the independent sector when he spoke of the disinclination of many independent schools to publish examination results, and went on to say that 'one reason why they fear a league table is that there are parts of the country (West Sussex for example) where maintained schools get better exam results than the independent schools, despite the former's non-selective entry'.

After 1992, when they were required to publish their results, the fact that the overall average was the crucial piece of information to be published had the effect of encouraging those schools to make their entry more selective in order to take only children who could be relied on to do well. A school such as Christ's Hospital, which existed to care for children in need and therefore admitted those most in need rather than the cleverest, could not help but slide down the league tables. A sixth form college such as Collyer's which took students over the whole range of ability would, however good the performance of its best candidates, necessarily have a lower average score than a selective school and be even lower in the league tables.

Meanwhile, the government continued with its policy of seeking to drive up standards in the post-16 sector by reducing funding, ostensibly in the belief that economy would lead to greater efficiency and effectiveness. The Further Education Funding Council implemented that policy on the one hand by reducing funding by about 8% a year, and on the other by diverting a substantial proportion of the already limited and reducing funding to setting up auditing and inspection systems by which they sought to clone colleges into competent mediocrity. Each college was required to produce a strategic plan, an accommodation strategy, a three year financial forecast and a self-assessment review. They all had to appoint both internal and external auditors. Everything needed to be evidenced, approved, monitored, validated, accredited, checked, inspected and audited.

It is a measure of the extreme nature of the regime that in a period of just two months they checked at Collyer's what were called our 'achievement units', they audited our operation of Adult Education, our financial systems and the provision of 'management information', inspected all eight of our curriculum areas, had external auditors 'validate' our Individual Student Records, and then had an FEFC auditor and an FEFC audit manager audit the work of our auditors and check our 'management systems', after which an FEFC accountant accompanied by a finance officer looked at our three-year financial forecast and considered the financial health of the college, before they audited our financial relationship with the local Training and Enterprise

Council, and finally had their inspectors look at the full range of what were called the cross-curricular areas of the college – and all within two months while the college went about its normal business.

We came out of it with a succession of reports that everything was in order and with the quality of the teaching in the college ranked second to only one other of more than six hundred colleges in the sector. But one could not help but get the impression that someone at the top was looking for trouble and expecting, even hoping, to find it. The extent and variety of the paperwork required was extraordinary, the cost both in money and time ludicrous, and, meanwhile, the demand to audit everything drove up the cost of auditors, which came out of the college budget, at the same time as our funding was being driven down.

It was particularly interesting to me that the one area in which were rated as low as 3 out of 5 was Quality Assurance. Everything else was apparently very good or outstanding, but not the system for achieving it. What the inspectors wanted was a Quality Assurance Committee which would measure everything and require improvements, while I believed that the key to success was highly motivated teachers who cared about and monitored the progress of individual students. You do not fatten pigs by weighing them, and you improve academic performance more by good teaching and guidance than by measuring results.

Meanwhile, despite the fact that central government had no policy for secondary education provision in the country as a whole and allowed local authorities to have a wide variety of different arrangements, civil servants at the centre tried to micromanage how a number of systems should operate in all secondary schools maintained out of the public purse.

In an attempt to have some central control over rates of truancy they prescribed in detail how all school and college registers were to be filled in, both morning and afternoon, with specified symbols for such things as an absence authorized because of a visit to the dentist, and a different symbol for a visit to a doctor. They prescribed the way in which school trips should be organized and specified the steps which would have to be taken towards cancelling such a trip when one of the projected group could not afford to pay and there was no hardship fund to cover the shortfall. Secretaries of State would make public pronouncements about such issues as the age at which they believed that primary school children should know their twelve times table.

But on the overall structure of the education service there was no hint of any strategic vision, and most Secretaries of State and Ministers with responsibility for Further and Higher Education clearly had little understanding of the arrangements over which they presided – understandably, because they usually held the position for so short a time. During my twenty-three years as a headmaster or college principal there were ten Secretaries of State, so the average time for which they held that post was just over two years. There were even more Ministers of State for Further and Higher Education, who would come from another department and either move on after a short while to yet another department or resign in order 'to spend more time with their families' – always before they had a real grasp of the issues facing them.

Neither the politicians nor the civil servants seemed to understand the practicalities of how schools operated. In 1986 the government and the teachers' unions rather extraordinarily agreed with each other to specify the number of hours that a teacher could be expected to work under the direction of and in a place designated by the head teacher. They settled on 1265 hours a year, those hours to be spread reasonably over thirty-six weeks, on thirty-five of which teachers could be expected to teach pupils.

But they did not make any provision for supervision during the lunch hour. So teachers in large comprehensive schools sometimes walked out for the duration of the lunch hour, leaving the head to supervise perhaps one and a half thousand teenagers, who might be perfectly well behaved when supervised, but were liable to be unspeakably awful if left day after day to their own devices. When representatives of the Secondary Heads' Association went to meet the relevant minister and his civil servants to explain how unworkable this was, they were met with the response from a senior civil servant, 'But don't you have string quartets and that sort of thing in the lunch hour? We used to at Harrow.'

For many years politicians appeared to have little or no interest in sixth form colleges, and neither Secretaries of State for Education nor Ministers of State for Further and Higher Education ever seemed to know much about them. They would proclaim the importance of the latest government initiative to 'drive up standards', but in such a way that it was sometimes clear that they did not know what they were talking about.

In the early 1990s John Patten, most remembered for his bouffant hair style and not to be confused with Chris Patten, was Secretary of State for Education under John Major. He spoke at an annual conference about the introduction of National Vocational Qualifications (or NVQs) and General National Vocational Qualifications (or GNVQs). 'The Prime Minister and myself', he said (his misuse of the reflexive pronoun causing a shudder among those with whom I was sitting), 'are entirely committed to NVQS and to GNVQS'. Unfortunately the secretary who had typed his speech for him had put a capital S in both cases, so that instead of saying 'NVQs and GNVQs' he had rattled off all the initials, including the capital Ss, making it clear that he did not know what he was talking about. Nor did he understand the laughter which followed.

One of the Ministers of State who coped best at an APVIC conference, the annual meeting of the Association of Principals of Sixth Form Colleges, had only been moved from Agriculture a couple of weeks earlier and had clearly been briefed that the answer to most questions he would face was that the government was committed to giving parents choice. So that was how he responded to most questions. I then explained that no comprehensive school in Horsham, whether boys', girls' or mixed, had a sixth form. Nor did we have a technical college or a community school or a city technology college or any other institution with a sixth form. My college, I explained, had a sort of monopoly of sixth form education in the town. What would the government be likely to do about that in order to provide parents with choice? He grinned and said, 'Who's a lucky boy then?', which seemed to me as good an answer as it was possible to give.

There was clearly an awareness in political circles that something was wrong with the arrangements for secondary education, or with the way they were operated, or both. So there were proposals for reforming the examination boards and the examination system. There were proposals for reforming the National Curriculum. There were proposals for reforming the inspectorate. There were proposals for reforming everything. There were new initiatives and new names for schools and even new Education Acts. But there was no attempt to tackle the need for a national system or the continuing problem of the relationship between the independent and the maintained sectors. Everything continued much as before.

In 1997, two years before I retired, the Labour Party won a general election, proclaiming that its policy was, 'Education, Education, Education', but they added that for their first two years in power they would live within the funding plans of the previous government. I had started as a headmaster in 1976, when funding cuts were imposed on the then Labour Government by the International Monetary Fund. I retired twenty-three years later, with another Labour government continuing the funding cuts which had for years been imposed with such enthusiasm by its predecessors. The Prime Minister and some of his colleagues spoke a lot about education, but they did not tackle the fundamental problems any more than their predecessors had, and they made no attempt whatever to find a way of integrating the independent and maintained sectors within one unified national system.

CHAPTER 17

The Accumulation of Problems

At this stage it may be worth summarising how the problems with English secondary education in the early twenty-first century had come about. They were largely the consequence of political interventions which had unfortunate, even if unintended, consequences. The encouragement given to the development of grammar schools throughout the country by the Education Acts of 1902 and 1918 was in itself admirable. But the arrangements for helping to fund them opened up the crucial divide between grammar schools, now funded, or partly funded, out of the public purse, and the public schools, which were independent of public funding.

Then the attempt in 1926 to clarify the grammar school funding arrangements produced the distinctions between 'direct grant', 'aided' and 'maintained' schools, while yet a further administrative category of 'voluntary controlled' schools was created by the 1944 Education Act. So long as those four different categories remained enshrined in law, as they did, coexisting with public schools, it was impossible to create a coherent system of secondary education even at local level – let alone nationally.

The 1944 Education Act was hailed as a great reform, but most parents were deprived of any choice over where and how their children should be educated, too few grammar school places were provided, and provision varied from one education authority to another. Most eleven-year-olds were humiliated by being treated as failures and directed to secondary modern schools, where they were given a curriculum unsuited to either their needs or their interests. The technical education which the Act promised was neglected in all but a very few areas. Worst of all, and despite the recommendations set out in the Fleming Report, nothing was done to integrate the public schools within a national system.

The imposition of the 11+ selection procedure throughout the country led to dissatisfaction with the selective system, and Circular 10 of 1965 heralded the destruction of most of the country's grammar schools. Many were swamped under the large secondary modern element with which they were mixed, most large towns were provided with comprehensive schools which were too big with sixth forms which were too small, and the confusion in the organisation of secondary education was increased as local education authorities adopted widely varying arrangements, many adopting a comprehensive system, others holding out against it, and yet others providing for a mixture of selective schools in some areas and comprehensives in others.

The decision by a Labour government in 1975 to put pressure on the direct grant and voluntary aided grammar schools to become comprehensives resulted in most of them joining the public schools, which were widely seen as socially superior, in the independent sector, which now increased significantly, both size and quality.

While the independent sector flourished, problems with comprehensive schools became increasingly obvious, and in 1980 the Conservatives introduced the Assisted Places Scheme to enable academically able middle-class children to escape their local comprehensive school. In doing so they boosted the independent sector further.

The establishment of a national curriculum in 1988 began a process of shifting power to the centre, so that by the twenty-first century Secretaries of State would be tempted to try to dictate just which books, plays and poems should be studied in English and which events should be studied in History. Since they had usually been educated in the humanities themselves and had little knowledge of maths and science, they were less likely to try to prescribe the details of mathematical and science syllabuses, and in subjects such as English and History most teachers could be relied on to subvert attempts to control just what they should teach and how they should teach it. But the threat of future political interference in the details of the curriculum is real and continues.

It was also in 1988 that O level was replaced by the General Certificate of Education. By then the examination system was no longer suitable for those high-achieving students for whom it had originally been designed. It was now intended to be appropriate for the whole range of ability and was designed so that most pupils could leave school with some qualification. But for academically weaker pupils, who were not necessarily lacking in ability in other areas, low grade academic qualifications were unrelated to anything likely to be of use in their subsequent careers, for which they were given no training.

The removal of sixth form colleges from local education authorities in 1992 prevented any more from being created, and thus a Conservative government frustrated the best solution which had yet been found to the problems which had arisen from comprehensive reorganization. The funding of sixth form colleges was reduced to a point at which a quarter were taken over by large, financially stronger, technical colleges.

Those which did survive did so with their funding per student so significantly reduced that when the average independent day school was charging fees of £16,000 a year and leading independent boarding schools were charging fees of £32,000, sixth form colleges were receiving funding of only about £4,000 per student. Strangely enough, the best sixth form colleges were still producing more A level passes and more high grades than were the leading independent schools, but they were doing it with large teaching groups and relatively few teachers, so that the government could make the savings required to cut taxes.

It was also in 1992 that the government required league tables to be published showing how schools were performing in public examinations. Not surprisingly those schools which regularly came at the top of the league tables were those with a selective intake, and the league tables which were a source of pride to selective schools, both the independent schools and the few remaining maintained grammar schools, were a source of humiliation to both pupils and teachers in many other schools and colleges – particularly those in difficult areas where they were struggling to cope in a system weighted against them.

In 1997 the New Labour government abolished the Assisted Places Scheme in the name of Equality, but it had no more idea than the Conservatives about how to tackle the now deeply engrained problems which had developed in English secondary education, many of them as a result of their own political interventions. Labour politicians were still, at least in theory, opposed to independent education, but they had no idea what to do about it and found it difficult to acknowledge that the problem now was very largely that so many independent schools were very good and had particularly well qualified staff, expensive facilities and impressive examination results. If the half century from the end of the First World War to the late 1960s had been the Golden Age of the grammar school, then the forty years after Labour gave its boost to the independent sector in 1976 was the Golden Age of the independent school, and it shows no sign of coming to an end.

In the late twentieth century one of the problems with 'state' secondary education in England was quite simply that there was a widespread sense that something was wrong. There continued to be no national system but instead a wide variety of provision from one local education authority to another, and wherever people lived they had little choice about which school or what sort of education their children should receive in their teenage years, unless they had the money to opt out of the 'state system' and send their child to an independent school.

In inner cities there are still too many large comprehensive schools covering the whole age range from eleven to eighteen. It is the fault of the system, not of the teachers or head teachers, that so many problems remain unresolved. One continuing problem is that some pupils in those schools appear to be seriously disruptive and scruffy by comparison with those at independent schools, and the assumption is easily made that independent schools know what they are doing and expect high standards, whereas 'state' schools are less well run and allow unkempt and untidy pupils to misbehave.

But the head of an independent school has ultimately the sanction of expulsion and can off-load pupils who persistently smoke and dress scruffily onto their local comprehensive, whereas the local comprehensive has a legal obligation to accept them and the head may need to spend a disproportionate amount of time coping with difficult pupils, and sometimes their even more difficult parents, who may claim a 'human right' to decide for themselves which rules should and should not be obeyed.

In the late twentieth century, and in the early years of the twenty-first, one government after another, dissatisfied with comprehensive schools but with little idea how to cope with what they sensed was a problem, thought up new sorts of schools as they tried to improve on what existed. After the City Technology Colleges came Community Schools, Grant Maintained Schools, Specialist Language Schools, Trust Schools and the rather grandly named University Technical Colleges. Faith Schools were applauded and Free Schools were encouraged. Any new initiative, it seemed, might persuade the voter that something was being done. 'Super-heads' were sent in to turn round failing schools.

Then Labour decided to tackle low standards in inner cities by removing their comprehensive schools from the control of local authorities and calling them Academies. The Conservatives decided to follow that by encouraging all schools to become Academies. From a political point of view, whether from the Left or the Right, anything was now better than a comprehensive school. But the continuing problem was that they were still in reality comprehensives, whatever they were called.

What all these schools had in common was that admission, at least in theory, was not selective and they were not allowed to charge fees. Usually they were provided with a higher level of funding than schools under local authority control, and in the twenty-first century the Conservatives steadily pursued a policy of removing as many schools as possible from local authorities, so that by 2015 three thousand schools scattered throughout England were operating under a direct contract with the Secretary of State.

A policy of trying to control everything from the centre, which had proved peculiarly inefficient when the Bolsheviks had tried, for example, to control soap production in the Uzbek Soviet Socialist Republic from Moscow, was now being adopted by a Conservative government in England. It tried to bypass local authorities, which it saw as obstacles to its plans, and manipulate schools from the centre. But it still did not set up the national system which was needed. What it provided was inefficient interference.

The interference made remarkably little difference. Whatever label was attached to their school, teachers continued to do the best they could. But the curriculum and the examinations up to the age of sixteen remained insufficiently demanding for high achievers and inappropriate for most of the rest, and the curriculum after the age of sixteen still combined the two faults of over-specialisation and too wide a range of courses, both of which resulted in serious gaps in both the knowledge and the understanding of many students.

The state of England's secondary education can, perhaps, be better illustrated by an analogy than by trying to describe it. Imagine a nationally sponsored athletics championship for teenagers, both girls and boys, with the competition designed to give selectors an opportunity to choose whom to select for the next level, the 18–21 age range. Each year ninety-three teams funded out of the public purse, though at widely varying levels, take part, and it is illegal for those training the teams to make any charge to the parents of the boys and girls taking part.

A few teams come from areas where team members are selected for their athletic ability, and there are some from clubs whose members are volunteers aged from sixteen to eighteen, but most come from a great mass of clubs which have what might be called a comprehensive intake and include all the local young people, who are required to take part, at least up to the age of sixteen, unless they have parents with enough money to opt them out. Many would rather have been doing something which would be a useful preparation for a job, or failing that, playing computer games or reading magazines. But they do not have a choice.

Each year when the national championships take place those ninety-three teams are joined by seven others which are entirely independent of the national system. They have their own admissions arrangements, the parents of those in the seven independent teams have been paying anything from about £15,000 to £35,000 a year for their children to be coached, and those who coach them are generally better paid than those who coach the other ninety-three teams.

When it comes to the selection process for those who will go on to the next level, about half of all who are chosen come from those seven teams, and of the other half a substantial number come from the relatively small number of teams from clubs with members chosen for their ability and from the large clubs with 16 to18-year-old volunteers. Meanwhile, progressive exponents of athletics try to drive up the standards of the great mass of teams by schemes for improving their coaching, by inspecting them and by trying to organise things better.

There is a limit to how far one should press an analogy, but England's arrangements for secondary education in the early twenty-first century are more or less as ludicrous as those arrangements for a national athletics competition. The independent schools educate about 7% of the nation's pupils in any one year and get about half the university places. It is not so very different.

The answer cannot sensibly be to do away with independent schools. With hindsight it looks as if most grammar schools were eliminated because they were too good to be acceptable. Their very excellence, sometimes described as élitism, was an offence to those yearning for an unattainable ideal of Equality. Now it is the independent schools which are too good, and even the most left-wing of politicians have abandoned any plans for trying to abolish them. That is understandable. It is less understandable that no politicians, whether on the left or on the right, appear to be trying to find a way of integrating the independent and maintained sectors.

Chapter 18

Towards a Solution

The task of the philosopher, said Wittgenstein, is to show the fly the way out of the fly-bottle. In this case the fly-bottle is English secondary education, with its bewildering confusions, its multifarious failings and above all the continuing, widening and damaging division between the independent and maintained sectors. That division both exemplifies and exacerbates the even more important division of English society between the rich and the poor. A way out has to be found and History, down the ages described as Philosophy teaching by examples, can provide examples which at least clarify the nature of the problem and lead towards a solution.

This investigation began with the striking difference between three schools charging boarding fees of more than £30,000 and another three forbidden by law from charging anything, although all six are engaged in the same activity of educating teenagers up to A level. The answer to how they came to be treated so differently has nothing to do with when they were founded. Two were sixteenth century foundations. One can and does charge fees; the other may not. Two were founded in the nineteenth century. One can and does charge fees; the other may not. Two were founded in the twentieth century. One can and does charge fees; the other may not.

Nor does the answer lie in the nature of their origins. Of the three independent schools Christ's Hospital was founded by a king and given a royal charter, while Clifton and Stowe were both founded by groups of individuals seeking to satisfy a perceived need. Of the three schools or colleges which since 1944 have not been allowed to charge fees, Collyer's was founded by an individual as an act of medieval piety and charity, QK has its origins in the beneficence of a Victorian philanthropist, and KGV was founded by a local government body. There is no simple answer for anyone wanting to understand the difference. The answer lies in the complicated history which has been explored in previous chapters and does not need repetition.

There were two occasions in the last one and a half centuries when there was an opportunity to create an integrated system of secondary education for England. The first was in 1869 when the Taunton Commission recommended setting up a national system based on the endowed grammar schools. Little was done.

The second came after half a century of piecemeal changes, by the end of which, at the end of the First World War, there was a fairly clear division between the boarding public schools and the day grammar schools. The difference between them, with the former charging roughly ten times as much as the latter, was so worrying to those concerned for social cohesion that the Fleming Committee was given the task of considering how the public schools might be integrated into a national system. Its recommendations in 1944 provided the second opportunity for creating an integrated system, but they were ignored and instead we got the 1944 Education Act.

If the public schools were not to be integrated into a national system, the one way of creating a truly national system was for the state to provide such successful schools, academic, technical and specialist, that most independent schools would not be able to survive in the face of the competition from the state sector. Again there were two opportunities for that.

The first was the period after the Second World War, when it should have been possible to develop the grammar schools, with all of them continuing to charge fees, but with a far larger number of free places than in the past. The direct grant grammar schools are an example of how that could have been done, but however it was done it should have been combined with the provision of technical schools as an alternative mode of secondary education. Instead the grammar schools came to be associated with the 11+ selection process and with meritocratic élitism, few technical schools were built, and most children were directed to unsatisfactory and underfunded secondary modern schools. Understandably that led to a nationwide demand for comprehensive schools.

The second opportunity was when large numbers of local education authorities, looking for a solution to the problems thrown up by comprehensive reorganisation, found it in the creation of sixth from colleges. Instead of pupils being divided by ability, as had happened widely in the past and still happens in some areas, they could instead be divided by age. That resulted in the possibility that good sixth form colleges, well-funded and well-staffed, would attract sixteen-year-olds away from their independent schools and erode the developing perception of a distinction between 'good' independent schools and 'bad' comprehensive schools.

But in 1976 the Labour government gave a massive boost to the independent sector by its ill-judged policy towards direct grant and voluntary aided grammar schools, and as a result of that misjudgement the independent sector grew both in size and quality. Subsequently the gap between the fees charged in independent schools and the funding per pupil received in the maintained sector grew ever wider. Then in 1992 a Conservative government adopted a policy towards sixth form colleges which prevented any more from being created, destroyed a quarter of those which already existed, and impoverished the rest.

Instead of having an impressive national system of academic, technical and specialist schools, England's arrangements for secondary education in the second half of the twentieth century remained confused, with the widely differing arrangements only becoming apparent to parents when they move from one part of the country to another. When they did, there was a significant probability that the arrangements in the area to which they were moving would be different from those in the area they were leaving.

In 2017 many of the major towns and cities of England, including London, still have comprehensive schools covering the age range 11–18. But in different parts of the country the starting age for secondary schools can be ten, eleven, twelve, thirteen or fourteen. In West Sussex, for example, all of those are possibilities, as a result of a policy of adopting whatever local arrangements were the least expensive.

Meanwhile, sixth form colleges are scattered, apparently at random, throughout the country and are independent of any local education authority. There are still 164 maintained grammar schools in England, spread over thirty-six local education authorities and educating about 4% of the country's children in any one year. Most are in Buckinghamshire, Lincolnshire and Kent. The rest are mostly in areas where the local authority maintains schools described as comprehensives, even though the academically brightest children are creamed off to the grammar schools.

The London Borough of Redbridge, where I grew up, will do as an example. Out of 152 education authorities in the country Redbridge is one of the three dozen which still have what is effectively an 11+ selection procedure, and that determines admission to two highly selective grammar schools: the Woodford County High School for Girls and the Ilford County High School for Boys. In Woodford there is also an independent, co-educational day school called Bancroft's, founded in 1737 by the Drapers' Company, and a comprehensive school known as Woodbridge High School.

Back in the early 1940s, when I lived down the hill in Woodford Bridge, I went to the elementary school in Snakes Lane called Ray Lodge which took children up to the age of eleven. A few children left a year early with a scholarship to go to a grammar school, but most went on to the senior section of the school in St Barnabas Road. Up until 1947 it was the senior section of an elementary school. After that, when the 1944 Education Act was implemented, it was a secondary modern school. Now the local authority describes it as a comprehensive school, even though the cleverest girls locally are creamed off to the Woodford High School for Girls, and the boys to Ilford, while those with parents who can afford it go to an independent school.

A couple living perhaps a quarter of a mile from Woodford Station in the prosperous area of Woodford Green, could well be more or less equidistant from, and not much more than half a mile's walk away from, all three: the Woodford County High School for Girls, Bancroft's and Woodbridge High School. If they have a particularly bright daughter and she passes the 11+, she could have high quality academic education free at the High School for Girls. If she fails the 11+, her parents would either need to find school fees of about £15,000 a year for seven years at Bancroft's (i.e. more than a hundred thousand pounds), or send her each day over to what a sociologist once described as the 'wrong side of the railway line', where she would go to Woodbridge High School. I remember that description of the railway line forming a social barrier because it was in an article I read when up at Oxford. I lived on the wrong side and understood what the author meant. I suspect it is still seen that way today.

That is not a criticism of Woodbridge High School, still less of the Woodford County High School for Girls or of Bancroft's. But it is most certainly a criticism of the system, and those arrangements are not significantly worse than those in most of England. It is neither typical nor especially unusual. Everything is arranged in accordance with the provisions of the 1944 Act and all subsequent acts. But no one would devise arrangements like that if starting from scratch. Something better is needed.

One of the greatest tragedies of the 1944 Act was that it very largely removed the opportunity for choice about their children's education from most parents. It removed the element of choice from the children as well. Another tragedy was the failure to build technical, or vocational, schools. Both of those failings are still waiting to be remedied.

After nearly three quarters of a century, in the early twenty-first century, the crucial division in secondary education is between those schools which charge fees and those which do not. That division goes back to decisions in the early twentieth century, when politicians unintentionally created a distinction between schools which received financial aid from public funds and those which were entirely independent. The divide became even wider as a result of the 1944 Education Act, which offered free secondary education to all and forbad the charging of fees to all publicly funded secondary schools except direct grant grammar schools.

It became wider still when in 1976 a Labour government unintentionally drove most of the direct grant and voluntary aided grammar schools into the independent sector, which then became both far larger and academically far more impressive than ever before. Since then the divide has become a chasm. The independent schools and the maintained schools and colleges still fulfil the same function of educating teenagers up to A level. But the fees of the independent schools have gone up faster than inflation, while funding in the maintained sector has been driven down so that the government can reduce taxes.

It is time to question the idea that everyone is entitled to free academic secondary education. Those with enough money to buy their own car can do so, but that does not mean that all public transport has to be provided free. Similarly those who can afford to buy their own house can do so, but that does not mean that all public housing has to be provided free. We charge people for using public transport and we expect those living in council houses to pay rent. So why should parents not be expected to pay something for their children's secondary education? Of course, some people get free travel and some get housing benefit. Similarly those with low incomes could have their child's school fees paid out of public funds.

As a society we want protection from foreign enemies and peace and stability at home. We also want good roads and railways, high quality medical and social care, and good schools. But at the same time we want lower taxes. The consequence has been that funding per pupil in secondary schools and colleges maintained out of public funds has been cut to about a quarter of the amount that some people pay for their child's education at a day school in the independent sector.

Conservative politicians argued that driving down funding in the maintained sector would result not only in economy but also in greater efficiency and effectiveness. They were not entirely wrong. Although they were not planning to make the public sector fit and lean enough to compete with the best independent schools in the open market, that is what they have achieved, and the time has come to develop a national system in which there is no distinction in law or in the provision of state funding for any schools which educate teenagers.

What is needed is a national policy, within which there is genuinely more choice for both parents and their children, with a curriculum appropriate to their needs, available to be chosen or rejected. Central government, with parliamentary approval, needs to determine a national system, but those who are responsible for the national strategy should avoid direct involvement in the details of local implementation. The implementation of the system should be in the hands of local education officers, but those officers should be responsible to central government rather than to local politicians for implementing national decisions.

Expenditure on education should be centrally funded, so that schools and the cost of teachers are no longer a charge on local taxation. Whatever funding arrangements are decided on should be applicable to schools generally. There must no longer be any distinction in law between independent and maintained schools. There needs to be a national plan for three stages of education between the ages of four and nineteen, with the outline curriculum at each stage determined nationally. But the planning for moving towards the national system, and arrangements for any necessary building work, can be devolved to local officers.

The biggest challenge is to politicians of all parties to put aside their long established assumptions about what is either desirable or possible and co-operate to create something on which they can agree and which will transform English education for the better.

CHAPTER 19

A Possible Answer

'The thing I like about David', said Margaret Thatcher, speaking of Lord Young, whom she had brought into her cabinet from industry, 'is that he brings me solutions, not problems.' So this is a suggested solution to the problem of how England could have an integrated national system of education. The age at which children transfer from one stage of education to another should be the same throughout the country. The distinction between independent and maintained schools should disappear. There needs to be high quality academic, technical and specialist education available for teenagers. Both they and their parents should have a large measure of choice about how they can best be prepared for adult life. Arrangements for state funding need to be determined nationally.

Responsibility for children's education rests in the first instance with parents, and parents need to accept that responsibility. The state exists to help its members – not to direct them. In the early years of a child's life, except in the case of children whose deprived circumstances require intervention, parents should be left to decide for themselves how to look after their children at home and when, for example, to send them to a nursery school. After that stage parents should still be free, as at present, to decide to educate their children at home or pay to have them educated privately. But most already choose to take advantage of the usually very good primary schools provided by local education authorities, issues to do with education are less of a problem at that stage than in later years, and the question of which school one went to at the age of seven is not socially divisive in adult life.

Almost everything in any proposal for an integrated national system will be open to argument and it needs to be clear that this is not a suggestion that there is only one possible way of doing it. But it is most certainly an argument that a fundamental reappraisal is needed of what schooling should be provided in the teenage years and of how schools catering for those years should be organised. The proposals set out here are an example of how to achieve that, and the starting point is that there should be three five-year stages in a young person's education: from four to nine, from nine to fourteen, and from fourteen to nineteen, though with the last year only for those who need and want it.

Primary schools should educate the age range four to nine, with the curriculum concentrating on the five Rs (Reading, Writing and Arithmetic, Right and Wrong) and on the five Arts: Music, Drama, Art, Physical Activities and Making Things. How that should be done can be left to the teachers, whose styles and interests will vary and who should so far as possible be freed to use their own judgement about the details of what to teach and how to teach it. Ideally the children should usually be actively engaged in their work and should become literate and numerate and practised in the use of computers, calculators and whatever new technology may be developed in the future. So far as possible their early experience of school should be enjoyable.

Subjects such as Physics, Chemistry and Biology, and even History and Geography, can be left until the children move on to the next stage of education in junior high schools, from the age of nine until fourteen. In these years the teaching of English and Mathematics will continue to be important and the curriculum should also include Technology and Information Technology, the Arts and recreational activities. The young should now be faced not only with subjects they enjoy but also with having to tackle some things which they may well not enjoy, and the principal aim at this stage should be to introduce them to subjects, both technical and academic, which they may wish to study later.

For the teenage years from fourteen to eighteen, and where necessary up to nineteen, what is needed is that young people should be free to choose either academic or technical education, or some specialist form of education, such as Music, Agriculture or Sports. They should also be free to choose not to go to school any longer but instead seek employment, with the option of returning to education later if they find that a poorly paid and boring job seems to offer no prospects for the future. The obligation should be on the schools to make what they provide attractive enough for students and their parents to choose it and be prepared, if necessary, either to pay for it or have their children demonstrate entitlement to a free place.

Technical schools need to provide for literacy and numeracy and training in a wide range of skills, accompanied by recreational activities and some general education. They should offer courses which lead to a range of options in the job market, rather than confining the students to learning one particular skill. Everyone needs some training in Information Technology. Many need some understanding of how to submit a quotation for a job and how to produce an invoice and keep accounts. If someone training as a plumber can also qualify as a heating engineer and as an electrician, as well as in secretarial skills and in bookkeeping, that is more valuable both to the individual and to society as a whole than having the experience of failure in studying academic subjects which are neither interesting nor useful.

Almost all secondary school teachers will remember pupils for whom low level academic education was entirely inappropriate but who would have engaged enthusiastically in a course which taught them something useful. They will also remember how bored teenagers could become disruptive and interfere with the education of those who enjoyed academic subjects. The fault was not so much with the teenagers as with the inappropriate curriculum to which they were subjected.

Academic schools covering the age range fourteen to nineteen would exist to provide for that substantial minority of young people who flourish on the study of academic subjects, and whose parents, rightly or wrongly, wish them to have that form of education. It is, and always has been, something of a luxury, and is attractive to some because of the presumption that it can lead to relatively well-paid and well-regarded employment later in life. In that sense it is vocational education, even if less obviously so than what is provided in a technical school.

Those choosing it should normally pay something towards it. Many parents could afford that if schools charged fees at about the level at which they are currently funded by the state, and anyone who cannot afford the fees should find that a free place, paid for either by the taxpayer or by the school or by a combination of the two, is available to those who can demonstrate that they are capable of benefiting from it.

It should be possible for teenagers to switch from one type of school to another, making use of the extra year, and all these schools should be independent of both central and local authority control, though the government or a local authority, as much as anyone else, could found a new school if it saw the need for one. The legal and charitable status of all 14–19 schools would be precisely the same, whether they were previously independent or maintained, comprehensive or selective. It would include most of what are at present independent schools, both boarding and day, sixth form colleges, the surviving grammar schools and those comprehensive schools (by whatever name they might be known) whose governing bodies opted for becoming an academic, technical or specialist school, rather than a junior high school. Just as students could choose which school they wished to attend, so the governing bodies of the schools could choose which students to accept.

There would need to be some form of national examination at the end of the junior high school course, so that the students and their parents would be well equipped to decide what form of education, if any, they would like to undertake next. The government would provide funding for free places at academic schools at a fixed national rate, but each school's governing body would decide for itself whether to offer as many as two hundred free places each year, or only half a dozen, or none. A school charging £35,000 a year would only get the same standard rate of funding for pupils offered a free place as a school charging as little as £5,000 and offering large numbers of free places.

Many independent boarding schools which already cover the 14–18 age range would need to change very little and their governing bodies would decide for themselves whether or not to offer any free places. Similarly a few comprehensive schools which already start at thirteen or fourteen would need to change very little, though they would of course now be responsible for their own funding and for making their own decisions about admissions policy. Many independent day schools and the surviving maintained grammar schools would need to lose their early years in order to keep to teaching only the years from fourteen upwards. The sixth form colleges would need to adjust to teaching the two years up to sixteen as well as the two years thereafter.

The government would set the level at which it was prepared to provide funds for free places offered at academic schools, and it could influence the size of the sector by the level at which it funded free places. Students might well find that some courses in technical schools were available free, funded by the government, a local authority or employers, because there was a demand for those trained in a particular skill, while for other courses their parents might need to pay all or some of the cost.

As in the past anyone (the monarch, for example, a London livery company, a local education authority, a successful business man or woman, a church or a football club) could found a new school, so long as they had the money to do so, as and when they saw a need. They could found day schools or boarding schools, or schools which were both. They could found academic, technical or specialist schools, single sex or mixed. They could provide boarding facilities or more extensive grounds for existing schools.

Although the governing body of any school would be able to decide whether or not to take boarders, it would not normally get from the government any more funding for a boarder than for a day pupil. Exceptions to that would include payment for the children of members of the diplomatic service or the armed forces serving abroad, but again the amount to be provided by the state should be at a fixed level and should not be determined by whatever fees the school charged. If a school charged more than the amount provided by the state, whether its fees were £30,000 or £10,000 or anything else, the parents would have to decide whether to pay the difference or send their child to another school whose fees were lower. Similarly, if and when the Social Services Department of a local authority wished to place a child in care in a boarding school, it would need to make a judgment about what could be afforded out of its budget.

With an integrated national system of secondary education every school could determine its own salary structure, subject to a requirement to express it by reference to a national scale. For example, a boarding school might advertise for a new member of staff to be paid on the national scale and be provided with free accommodation, while a day school might advertise for a head of department, offering to pay significantly more than the national scale because the school was in central London.

It could be helpful to have a central staffing or appointments board charged with encouraging teachers to broaden their experience and encouraging schools to simplify the process of job applications by having a standard *curriculum vitae* format, so that anyone applying for another post should not have to waste hours filling in a range of differing forms. All schools should be subject to a national system of inspection, preferably with inspections at short notice to observe and report on what was good and what was bad. But these are all details.

The important thing is the development of an integrated system of education for the whole country.

With such a system the range of career opportunities available to teachers would be extended. Depending on their own background, qualifications and interests, some would confine their careers to primary, junior high, technical, academic or specialist schools. But it would be possible for someone to start as a teacher in any of those types of school, move after a few years to a post as a local education authority officer, return to teaching, perhaps as a head of department, and on to some years in the inspectorate before becoming a head teacher and maybe spending the last years of a varied career working in the Department of Education.

A reform such as I have outlined here would probably only be possible with cross-party agreement and legislation to require local authorities to implement the arrangements. It would be difficult but not impossible. Politicians of all complexions would need to change deeply ingrained attitudes. But the alternative is an ever widening gulf between an expensive independent sector educating the talented children of the international super-rich, and a poorly funded state sector whose schools and colleges are required to seek to educate the remaining 93%, giving few of them the high quality academic, technical or specialist education from which they could benefit, and providing most with a low level academic education which is neither of interest nor benefit to them.

By the Law of Unintended Consequences the policies of a Labour Government in 1976 helped to create large numbers of academically impressive independent schools which are too good to be abolished. By the same law Conservative funding reductions since 1992 have made many maintained schools and colleges far more cost-effective than independent schools. It is time to let them compete in the open market.

CHAPTER 20

Epilogue

The involvement of politicians in secondary education in the twentieth century usually did more harm than good, and worst of all they exacerbated the problem of the divide between the independent and maintained sectors. In a lifetime during which I moved backwards and forwards between the two sectors I could not help but notice both the differences and the similarities. Of the fifty years of my life spent in schools which teach teenagers up to A level, twenty were in three schools which remained independent of political control, and thirty in another three which, by the time I became a schoolmaster in 1957, were funded entirely out of the public purse and, for better or for worse, were later altered out of all recognition.

The three independent schools were Christ's Hospital, Clifton College and Stowe. They were relatively little affected by government education policy, and in the seventy years after the Second World War their fees rose until by the end of 2015 each of them was charging over £30,000. The other three were Collyer's in Horsham, Quintin School in St John's Wood, London, and King George V School, Southport. They were all grammar schools during the first decade of my teaching career, but Quintin became a comprehensive in 1967, while Collyer's and KGV both became sixth form colleges in the 1970s.

What all six of these schools had in common was more important in the years between the wars than their differences. Each was aiming to provide high quality education to teenagers, and they were all in the business of providing upward social mobility. The three grammar schools charged fees in the range of £15–£20 a year for day pupils, an amount affordable by many of the middle classes, and they gave scholarships to provide free places to bright children whose parents could not afford the fees. Christ's Hospital, as an ancient charitable institution with substantial endowments, educated only those whose parents' income was low enough for them to need free education. Clifton and Stowe charged boarding fees in the range from £150–£200 a year.

There was always something of a divide between public schools and grammar schools and no doubt many pupils of Clifton and Stowe, in common with public schoolboys generally, saw themselves as socially superior to pupils at grammar schools, while many of the pupils of the three grammar schools would have seen themselves as academically superior to those who attended public schools. Old Blues, the former pupils of Christ's Hospital, were conscious of the privilege of having attended a distinguished charitable institution and had their own sense of superiority. We were sometimes, perhaps, guilty of a form of inverse snobbery, and Roy Hattersley, at one time Deputy Leader of the Labour Party, said that 'Christ's Hospital is worse than the other public schools. They just perpetuate privilege; Christ's Hospital creates it.'

It is worth looking at how each of them was affected by government policy, starting with the three which are now publicly funded. The oldest of all the six, Collyer's, was founded in the early sixteenth century. It was independent of political control until the 1902 Education Act arranged for its running costs to be paid by the local education authority, and in the middle of the twentieth century it was a voluntary aided grammar school. In 1976 it became a sixth form college and had the considerable benefit of the Collyer Endowment, which was held by the Mercers' Company and, being valued at about £300,000 in the early 1990s, was worth some two million pounds, since the foundation only had to pay 15% of the cost of any new buildings. But when the government moved Collyer's into the new Further Education sector in 1992 it also removed it from the voluntary aided provisions and effectively slashed the value of the Collyer Endowment by about one and three quarter million pounds. A quarter of a century later the college remains under political pressure to deliver good results as cheaply as possible.

The Regent Street Polytechnic Day School, founded in the heart of London in 1886, the fruit of Victorian philanthropy, was also, like Collyer's, provided with public funding under the terms of the 1902 Act, and that began the process by which it changed from 'aided' to 'controlled' when it needed a new building after the Second World War. That in turn meant that the Inner London Education Authority was able to destroy it as a grammar school and turn it into a comprehensive school in 1967.

As Quintin Kynaston, or QK, it needed decades to emerge from the disaster into which it was plunged, but by the end of the century enough progress had been made that in 2001 it was designated a Specialist Technology College and proclaimed a model of a successful comprehensive school. In 2002 a new headteacher, Jo Shuter, was appointed, lauded as a 'superhead', proclaimed 'Headteacher of the Year in a Secondary School' in 2007, and awarded a CBE in 2008. The prime minister, Tony Blair, described the school as 'a wonderful inspiration', it received glowing Ofsted reports in 2004 and in 2008 and in 2011 became a Community Academy, independent of its local education authority, the Borough of Westminster, and responsible for its budgeting and accounting processes only to parliament. The headteacher had an annual salary of £170,000.

Then allegations of financial impropriety led to an investigation by the Education Funding Agency and a report showed that since QK had become an academy, more than £3,000 had been spent on flowers, £7,000 on taxis and another £7,000 on the headteacher's fiftieth birthday party. Seven members of her family had been employed at the school, including her mother and her children, and the final recommendation of the report was that the school's resources should not be spent on arranging aspects of the head's personal life, 'such as booking family holidays, organising the rental of her Turkish villa and on lunch and dinner engagements'. Somehow a highly regarded headteacher had been seduced into a self-indulgent life style paid for by claiming expenses in a manner characteristic of the worst elements of political and business life. She had to go.

In the twenty-first century QK was expensively rebuilt as the government poured money into rescuing the inner London comprehensives, and by 2015 it had nearly a thousand and a half pupils on roll, with nearly four hundred in the sixth form. But it still faces the problem that, despite laudatory OFSTED reports and an atmosphere of purposeful activity, its A level results are below the national average, and most parents living nearby sent their children to independent schools. That is likely to continue so long as QK remains a comprehensive school, but it is possible to imagine it having a successful future as a first-rate 14–18 technical school, providing a valuable alternative form of secondary education in the London Borough of Westminster.

King George V School had been founded by the burghers of Southport in 1920 to provide the town with a boys' grammar school. They were responding to the 1918 Education Act, and the new school was maintained with some pride while Southport had its own local education authority. After 1944, of course, it was no longer allowed to charge fees and its intake was determined by the 11+ examination. It grew in numbers and held out for about a decade against the comprehensive movement until local government reorganisation in 1974 moved Southport from Lancashire to be part of Merseyside and some secondary education reorganization became necessary.

Fortunately the change, when it came, was a rational and sensible arrangement. KGV became a mixed sixth form college and a model of 'a grammar school at 16+'. But in 1992 it was moved into the Further

Education sector and by the end of the century its income per student was reduced to the point at which it was a quarter of the level of the income per student of the neighbouring former direct grant schools. Then political and financial pressures drove it to undertake educational functions which would have been better left to the technical college only a mile away. Although up till the end of the first decade of the twentieth century it was still being held up by the inspectorate as a model of a good college, cuts in funding had the effect that a few years later it was being described by Ofsted as 'inadequate' and in 2017 arrangements were made for it to merge with Southport College, formerly the Southport Technical College.

While the three former grammar schools had been significantly changed by political intervention, the independent schools were relatively unscathed, though not entirely. The oldest of them, Christ's Hospital, founded in London twenty years after Collyer's, was a charity, a 'dede of pittie', caring for the children of the poor, and when I went there in 1944 it was an essential qualification for entry that one's parents' income should be below an income bar, so that they could not afford to pay any fees.

In 1867 the Taunton Commissioners had described it as 'a thing without parallel in this country, and *sui generis*' (i.e. unique), 'a grand relic of the medieval spirit – a monument of the profuse munificence of that spirit'. It suffered in 1965 from the decision of the newly formed Inner London Education Authority that it would no longer provide for London children who had done well in the 11+ to go there, and in 1987 it also suffered from the withdrawal of the Assisted Places Scheme.

But both of those things were trivial compared with the damage done to its endowment by inflation in the second half of the twentieth century and by a collapse in the value of its property and investments. The Almoners, who governed the foundation, tried to carry on as before, as if nothing had happened, and early in the twenty-first century they were spending two million pounds a year more than their income on the recurrent funding of the school and more millions on building and refurbishment work. Then their investments were hit by the banking crisis of 2007–8, and they resorted to taking full fee-payers to prop up the hospital's finances, so that by 2014 there were as many parents paying full fees as those who paid nothing. Instead of the children being housed, clothed and educated free, their parents were now awarded bursaries as a percentage of the full boarding fees of over £30,000.

The scale on which those bursaries were awarded was so great that, of the sixty million pounds worth of bursaries provided by the 274 HMC independent schools in 2014 to high-performing children to enable them to escape from their local comprehensive school, more than a quarter of that sum came from Christ's Hospital. But only time would tell if it could retain its charitable mission or if financial pressure would gradually change it into one more expensive public school, like so many charitable foundations before it.

Clifton College, founded in an attractive suburb of Bristol in the mid nineteenth century, had always had day boy houses and was the first school in the country to join the Assisted Places Scheme introduced by a Conservative government in 1980. It adjusted its admissions policy accordingly. Then in 1997, when a Labour government abolished the scheme, it had to adjust again and returned to complete independence. It continued to flourish, and in the early twenty-first century was another of that small group of leading public schools able to charge fees of over £30,000.

The last to be founded of the six schools at which I spent fifty years of my life was Stowe. Just as KGV was an expression of the demand for more grammar schools after the First World War, Stowe was an expression of the desire for more high quality public schools, and as a new school it was able to develop a different ethos from that of most public schools. Housed in the magnificent building which had once been the home of the Dukes of Buckingham, and surrounded by

750 acres of landscaped gardens, it had a spectacular rise to become one of the country's leading boarding schools. Its image gradually changed from that of a country club, with a beagle pack and a golf course, to that of a school set in a strikingly attractive environment, academically successful and able to compete in every way with the best schools in the country. In 2014, when it opened its new Music School costing £7,000,000, it was having no difficulty in attracting pupils whose parents could afford to pay more than £30,000 a year.

Christ's Hospital, Clifton and Stowe are all three strikingly successful schools where parents who can afford high fees are pleased with what they provide. Meanwhile, Collyer's, QK and KGV between them produce more A level results, and more good A level results, than the combined results of Christ's Hospital, Clifton and Stowe, and the education they provide costs the students' parents nothing.

The differences between these six schools and their similarities form a commentary on the fundamental problem with English secondary education which politicians of all parties avoid facing – the problem of the relationship between the independent and maintained sectors. It is a problem affecting the whole of society. If things continue much as they have for the last half century, it is likely that within another decade Christ's Hospital, Clifton and Stowe will be educating the charming, attractive, intelligent and talented children of the international super-rich, and sending them on to the best universities and to well-paid and influential jobs in finance, politics, law and the BBC, while Collyer's, QK and KGV will be struggling to survive, as politicians, seeking to cut taxes while finding money for health, defence, infrastructure and pensions, drive their funding ever lower.

If, on the other hand, politicians can throw off their deeply ingrained party political assumptions and co-operate to find a way of integrating the maintained and independent sectors, it is perfectly possible that all six, and innumerable other schools as well, will be able to operate on the same terms, with equal status in law and an equal right to attract public funding for free places, in a coherent national system providing high quality academic, technical, vocational and specialist education for all who want it.

Index